NATHAN THE WISE

Patriach worst characte-
is intolerant.

Dara — is also somewhat
intolerant

Templar — starts out intolerant
and becomes increasingly
tolerant because of
his ~~and~~ relationship
with Nathan and
Sultan sparing him.

Man is important,
not religion.
The sectarian titles
don't mean anything

Humanity is most important

Compliments of the GERMAN INFORMATION CENTER

GOTTHOLD EPHRAIM

LESSING

NATHAN THE WISE

TRANSLATED WITH AN INTRODUCTION
BY WALTER FRANK CHARLES ADE
Ed.D., Ph.D., F.I.A.L.
PURDUE UNIVERSITY

BARRON'S EDUCATIONAL SERIES, INC.

All inquiries should be addressed to:
Barron's Educational Series, Inc.
113 Crossways Park Drive
Woodbury, New York 11797

Library of Congress Catalog Card No. 73-179722

International Standard Book No. 0-8120-0140-0

To my dear wife

ELEANOR ANNE ADE

on the occasion of our

thirtieth wedding anniversary

June 1941 — June 1971

To my dear wife

INTRODUCTION

A number of excellent biographies of Gotthold Ephraim
Lessing (1729-1781), along with critical studies of
his literary activities and works, have appeared in
English, so that a detailed examination of his life
and works would be superfluous here. A chronological
list of his literary products is given at the end of
this Introduction and a selected bibliography will be
found after the Appendix. Here the writer will, therefore, limit himself to a general sketch of Lessing's
brief life of fifty-two years, to a short explanatory
comment on his two great critical works, the *Laocoön*
and the *Hamburg Dramaturgy* and to a more detailed
examination of his last great dramatic effort, *Nathan
the Wise*, which is herewith presented in a modern
English translation.

Gotthold Ephraim Lessing was born on January 22,
1729, the son of a Lutheran clergyman, at Kamenz in
Saxon Lusatia. He was thus a contemporary of Voltaire
and the French *philosophes*, of Frederick the Great
and his academy of scholars in Berlin, and—later in
life—of the young Goethe and Schiller. He was born
into the Age of Reason (the English Age of Enlightenment and the German *Aufklärungsperiode*) in eighteenth-
century Europe. It was an era when rationalism
reigned supreme, when all things were subjected to the
cold, hard logic of reason, when anything that could
not be understood and clarified by this process was
rejected. It was an age of atheism and deism which
in France finally deprived the nobility and the Church
of their hereditary feudal powers and witnessed the
rise of the *tiers état*, the masses. It was also the
age of the Seven Years' War, the American Revolution,
and the French Revolution, which began shortly after

Lessing's death. The German Storm and Stress Movement in literature unfolded in the later years of his
life and in 1779, the year in which *Nathan the Wise*
was given to the world, Goethe also completed his
Iphigenie auf Tauris in rhythmic prose, a work which
was ultimately to become the finest example of the
German classic drama.

In 1741 Lessing entered the St. Afra School for
Princes (Fürstenschule) in Meissen, and already here
in this fine secondary school he received a rich and
thorough humanistic education. After completing his
program at this school, in 1746 he matriculated to
the University of Leipzig, where he set out to study
theology and actually graduated from this school with
a Master of Arts degree in theology. At Leipzig he
discovered, however, that "books might make him
learned, but could never make him a man." Gradually
he became more and more imbued with the spirit of
rationalism and enlightenment, with the social life
in Leipzig, and with the theatre, this last due chiefly to the great influence which Madame Neuber and her
theatrical company exerted upon him. The result was
that he decided to abandon theology and earn his
living as a free-lance writer.

From 1748 until 1760 Lessing was active in Berlin
most of the time as a journalist and an author.
While there, he formed lasting friendships with men
such as Friedrich Nicolai, the well-known bookdealer
and rationalist; Moses Mendelssohn, whom he later im-
mortalized as the prototype of his Nathan; Ewald von
Kleist, a Prussian officer in the armies of Frederick
the Great, who fell in the Seven Years' War at the
Battle of Kunersdorf; and other scholarly men with
rationalistic views. In Berlin he also made the ac-
quaintance of Voltaire, who was regarded in the court
circles of Frederick the Great as the greatest man of
the age. Lessing admired Voltaire at this time, but
he did not submit blindly to him if he deemed him in

error. The author of *Nathan the Wise* was, in fact,
already applying his keen critical faculty to religion. He had drifted with other scholars far in the
direction of the fashionable deism of the age, but
his fighting spirit was aroused no less by the over-
confident enemies of Christianity than by its over-
zealous and bigoted orthodox defenders. Lessing
stated the matter as follows: "The more rigorously
the one side tried to prove their Christianity, the
more doubtful I became; and the more arrogantly and
triumphantly the other side undertook to trample it
underfoot, the more I felt inclined to maintain it,
at least in my heart." Surely his abhorrence of
religious charlatanism and sham is already abundantly
evident here, as is the idea that religion abides in
the hearts of men, not in sterile, narrow-minded
dogma!

  Next Lessing served as secretary to the Prussian
Lieutenant-General von Tauentzien in Breslau for some
years and then returned to Berlin. Finding himself
temporarily without a livelihood at this time, in
1767 he journeyed to Hamburg, where he held the post
of dramaturgist or writer on dramatic theory and art
in the newly founded Hamburg National Theatre for one
year until it folded up. In 1770 he held the official position of ducal librarian in Wolfenbüttel.
Here he married the widowed Eva König of Hamburg in
1776 but lost his dearly beloved wife a year later in
childbirth, the child also dying on Christmas Day,
1777, before the mother. Lessing's five letters sent
from Wolfenbüttel to his friend, Professor Joachim
Eschenburg, in Brunswick between December 31, 1777,
and January 14, 1778, show his heart-rending grief
and shock as well as his despair and resignation.
Physically broken and almost blind, he died on
February 15, 1781, while on a visit in Brunswick.

  Throughout his life Lessing was engaged in controversies mostly literary and religious. He abhorred

sham and mediocrity and time after time he fought his
foes with the hard cold logic of rationalistic truth
which could not be denied. Often he found himself a
lone pioneer in the wilderness and he was indeed
worthy in every respect of the epithet "der grosse
Aufklärer" (the great enlightener). Two critical
works make him outstanding, the *Hamburg Dramaturgy*
and the *Laocoön*. In the former, more than any other
man, he brought German dramatic art into proper focus,
turning to English rather than to French drama for
guidance and, in so doing, he heralded the Golden Age
of German Classicism of Goethe and Schiller in Weimar.
His *Laocoön*, likewise a masterpiece of clear, logical
thinking, established for all time the boundaries
which separate and delimit the provinces of poetry
and the plastic arts in such a manner as to prove the
necessary futility of minute description in the former, poetry, and of symbolism in the latter, the
plastic arts.

The man who was responsible for awakening this interest in Hellenism in Germany at that time was
Johann Joachim Winckelmann, whose enthusiastic de-
scriptions of ancient Greek statues in his *History of
the Art of Antiquity* (Dresden, 1764) opened up new
vistas both in archeology and in art criticism and was
a main motivating force for Lessing and also for
Goethe. "Why," Winckelmann asks, "does Laocoön appear
nobly calm in the statue, whereas Virgil makes him
scream with pain in the *AEneid*?" His answer is that
this is completely in order because, like all Greek
statues, this one gives expression to the ethical
ideal of "noble simplicity and silent grandeur."
Lessing, however, contends that the sculptor was not
concerned with ethics, but with physical beauty. In
typical eighteenth-century fashion he then develops
his thesis with logical ratiocination, so that the
following dogma emerges from his analysis. The very
nature of the means employed by poetry and plastic
art respectively demands that the latter be confined

to the representation of things co-existent in space,
that is, bodies; while the former must necessarily
represent things sequent in time, that is, actions.
Obviously, according to Lessing, it follows from this
premise that the descriptive poet who attempts to give
a vivid impression of an object by describing its individual parts, one after the other, must fail, because the mind can never synthetize all the details
into a simultaneous all-at-once impression. While
Lessing's argument in the *Laocoön* is vulnerable in
some respects, it is none-the-less one of the most
stimulating pieces of criticism ever written. The
clarity and cogency of his logic are superb and probably its greatest importance at that time and since is
the "ferment of thought," as its author expressed it,
that it has produced in other minds. Goethe, for instance, described the effect it had on himself and
his contemporaries in the following words: "Like a
flash of lightning the consequences of this splendid
thought lighted up the way before us, and all previous
criticism was thrown away like a worn-out coat."

Lessing's *Hamburg Dramaturgy*, his second great
critical work, has the value of a classic treatise on
dramatic art, though in form it was a weekly journal
conducted in connection with the newly formed Hamburg
National Theatre which soon folded up. Lessing's
hypothesis is that it is possible to arrive at absolute
canons of art and that the way to do it is to study
the Greeks. His position toward French Classical
Drama in particular is that of a keen and resourceful
attorney for the prosecution. Voltaire—Lessing's
rival—is subjected to a withering criticism; Shakespeare is exalted. Furthermore, Lessing shows that
the restrictive rules of the French *haute tragédie*
are really mere pedantries for the most part, based
on a misinterpretation of Aristotle, their supreme
authority. Actually, Lessing was probably less concerned with a disparagement of French Classical Drama
than in disillusioning its German imitators. What he

was chiefly bent on shattering, however, was the fact
that French Classical Drama was not satisfied to stand
on its own merit as French, but claimed—at least in
the statements made by its lawgiver Boileau—to be
Greek. Had the French been content to pride themselves in having produced a noble and stately form of
dramatic art which was thoroughly French, Lessing
would probably not have objected nearly as vehemently.
But when this French form and style and these French
rules were falsely paraded as being genuinely Greek,
so much so that they had become a hampering influence
to contemporary German dramatists, Lessing decided
that he must put the whole matter in its proper focus
in order to enlighten his credulous countrymen. The
reader cannot but feel that for Lessing the merit of
Shakespeare is not so much in being Shakespeare as it
is in being a better Greek than Voltaire or Corneille.
In a word, the times demanded a clear-sighted judicial
appraiser, but even more than that Lessing's Germany
demanded a liberator to tear off the false mask of
Hellenism in the French Classical Drama. It remained
for Lessing to unmask this pseudo-Hellenism, and he
did it very convincingly.

In the valedictory issue of the *Hamburg Dramaturgy*,
Lessing wrote his own well-known renunciation of the
name of inspired poet in the sense that Goethe was a
living exemplification of the term. Later on,
Schiller did much the same thing in his essay *Concerning Naive and Sentimental Poetry*, in which he compares
himself and Goethe as poets. Lessing explained that
he did not feel the living spring of poetry within
him and claimed that whatever success he had enjoyed
as a poet he owed solely to his critical faculty. It
was because of this opinion that Lessing was annoyed
to hear the critical faculty belittled. "There are
some who state that it stifles genius," he wrote,
"and I thought I had got something from it, something
that comes very close to genius. I am a lame man who
cannot possibly be edified by a lampoon against

crutches." In passing, it should be noted that
Emilia Galotti, the second of his three best-known
plays, is probably most accurately described as a
tragedy sired by the critical intellect, but one so
keen and so well disciplined that it almost deserves
to be called genius. Although its catastrophe is
somewhat dubious and shocking, *Emilia Galotti* is,
nevertheless, an excellent example of closely knit
dramatic construction. The characters are lifelike,
there is rapid vital movement, excellent motivation,
and every sentence has its own import.

What many critics believe to be Lessing's greatest
work, namely *Nathan the Wise*, will now be considered.
This work he called "the son of his old age, whom
polemics helped to deliver." In 1779, three years
before his death, Lessing delivered the weightiest
message of his stormy career in the form of what he
was pleased to call "a dramatic poem", a work which
deals with religious and racial tolerance and humane
aspiration and brotherhood. In this play Lessing
concentrated on this noble message rather than on the
sound principles of dramatic construction, even though
the latter are very much in evidence too. Before
proceeding with a critical analysis of *Nathan the
Wise*, a few remarks must be devoted to the events
which were responsible for the writing of this great
and noble work.

Soon after the debacle of the Hamburg National
Theatre, Lessing accepted from the Duke of Brunswick
the post of ducal librarian at Wolfenbüttel, and it
was here in the seclusion of this library that he
soon became involved in a religious controversy to
which he devoted most of his mental energy for the
remainder of his life. In the course of his duties
as librarian, he had come across a bulky manuscript
which attacked the credibility of the Bible. The
author of this highly controversial treatise entitled
Apology for the Sensible Worshippers of God was a

Hamburg Orientalist, Hermann Samuel Reimarus, who had
recently died. Reimarus had devoted many years to
this work, but he had not published it because he had
reached conclusions which were bound to shake the
very foundations of Lutheran orthodoxy. Although
Lessing could not agree with Reimarus on every point
of his argument, he was impressed by the gravity and
acumen of his logic. It did not take Lessing long to
come to the decision that the pursuit of truth is
better than a sure conviction that one already has it,
and so he made up his mind to publish extracts from
the manuscript under the title of *Anonymous Fragments*.
The result was utter consternation in the ranks of
the orthodox clergy. A Hamburg pastor by the name
of Goeze responded by vigorously attacking Lessing,
over the head of the *Great Anonymous*, as an enemy of
religion. Lessing then replied in a series of pamphlets which constitute a brilliant vindication of
what is now called the higher criticism. Among other
things, he argued that religion is older than the
Bible and cannot, therefore, be based solely on the
Bible. Moreover, he argued that the truth of religion must be proved, not by historical logic, but
rather by its effect on the character of its devotees.
This bitter theological controversy was growing
hotter every day, and Lessing had just finished the
eleventh chapter of his withering *Anti-Goeze* when the
orthodox party was successful in persuading the Duke
of Brunswick to silence his "godless" librarian by
official decree. Lessing was informed that his
writings were subversive in that they opposed "the
principal doctrines of Holy Writ and Christianity"
and that he was forbidden to publish any more such
"anti-orthodox" pamphlets. Immanuel Kant was told
the same thing sixteen years later by the Prussian
Ministry.

In the summer of 1778 Lessing then conceived the
idea of stating his case in a dramatic poem. To
Elise Reimarus he wrote: "I must see whether they

will at least let me preach undisturbed from my old
pulpit, the stage." To his brother and to Moses
Mendelssohn he wrote, that he had come across the
sketch of an old play made by him years ago, and that
he was going to finish it "in order to play a better
joke on the theologians with this play than he could
with ten *Anonymous Fragments* more." His friends
naturally expected something very severe and satiri-
cal, until he enlightened them with his *Nathan*. The
work has a twofold connection with the theological
quarrels. Previously Lessing had attacked his enemies
keenly and mercilessly. Now he heaped coals of fire
upon their heads by writing a work that breathes the
very spirit of toleration and love throughout! This
was indeed a strange revenge! Not that it was viewed
in that light, except by a very few. Again, due to
Lessing's disinterested love of the truth and of fair
play, exhibited during the controversies, he was in
danger of losing his position and his livelihood. A
note of three hundred thalers became due, and he
needed money to pay it. He did so by giving to the
world *Nathan the Wise*, which was published the following May by subscription.

The nucleus or *Kernpunkt*, as the Germans call it,
of the whole play is the tale of the three rings.
Lessing set this jewel of a story in his *Nathan* by
inventing for it an "episode", as he calls it. He
found it in Boccaccio's *Decamerone*, Day 1, Story 3.
But Boccaccio was not the originator of this tale,
which is thought to be of Oriental origin. It has,
in fact, a long and interesting history and passed
from one country to another, changing both in form
and in meaning in the various versions which have
come down to us. The first recorded version is found
in Spanish-Hebrew literature about 1100, its authorship being ascribed to a Spanish Jew. It has been
preserved in Rabbi Salome ben Verga's *Schebet Jehuda*,
a collection of tales made at the close of the fifteenth century. The next earliest account of this

famous Ring Parable appeared in the *Cento Novelle
Antiche*, a widely-known twelfth-century collection of
Italian stories, in which version the tale is perhaps
the oldest, since it is the simplest and shortest.
From here the story passed into the *Gesta Romanorum*,
a collection of Latin tales compiled in the early
thirteenth century, one of its three versions con-
taining an important additional trait which Lessing
used, namely that the true ring has the power of
making its wearer beloved by God and man. In 1311
Busone da Gabbia, a contemporary of Dante, included
the tale in his novel entitled *Avventuroso Siciliano*,
but it is not definitely known whether Busone took his
version of the Ring Parable from the *Cento Novelle
Antiche* or elsewhere. It is, however, certain that
Boccaccio made use of various incidents in Busone's
tale but that in general he does not deviate greatly
from other Italian accounts. Boccaccio's fourteenth-
century version comes next chronologically and it was
chiefly from Boccaccio that Lessing in 1779 drew for
his version in *Nathan the Wise*, but refining and ex-
panding the parable so that it became much more meaningful in his beautiful drama. Accounts of the
various versions of the Ring Parable have been recorded in some detail in authoritative English
translations in an Appendix, which will be found
after Act V of this translation of *Nathan the Wise*.
It should be noted that scholars do not agree as to
the first origin of the Ring Parable, a question
which is fully treated by Dr. A. Wünsche, Erich
Schmidt, and Gaston Paris in their works which have
been included in the Bibliography.

According to Boccaccio's mediaeval Italian version,
Saladin was once in urgent need of money and set a
trap for a wealthy Jew named Melchisedech by asking
him which was the best of the three religions. The
Jew skilfully extricates himself by telling the
famous ring story. Boccaccio's ring is merely a
very valuable jewel, which the head of the house

regularly bequeaths to the favorite son who is to
succeed him as head. At last it comes to a father
with three sons who are equally obedient and equally
beloved. Unwilling to choose among them, the father
has two new rings fashioned, so exactly like the
original ring that he himself can scarcely distinguish
them. He gives a ring to each of his three sons and
dies. Each son naturally claims to be the head of the
house, but there is no way of deciding which one of
the three has the genuine ring, and so "the question
which was the father's very heir abode pending and
yet pendeth." Thus ends the tale as told in the
Decameron, where the chief emphasis falls on the
shrewdness of the Jew.

By means of two happy additions, Lessing changed
the story in such a way as to give it an infinite
depth of symbolic suggestion and to make it embody
his whole philosophy of religion. In the first place,
he assigns to the genuine ring the magic power to
make its possessor beloved of God and man. The ring
in one version in the *Gesta Romanorum* was also said
to have that power, but Lessing adds a condition:
provided it be worn with faith in its efficacy. Sec-
ondly, he has the quarreling sons take their dispute
before a wise judge, who first reprimands them for
their contentiousness, and then, declaring that he is
unable to solve their riddle at the present time, he
looks forward to a time in the future, a thousand
thousand years hence, when a wiser judge may possibly
be able to render a decision.

It becomes evident that *Nathan the Wise* regards
religion from the point of view of evolution. Its
doctrine is a much finer matter than the prevailing
eighteenth-century doctrine of tolerance, which was,
in fact, compatible with a cynical contempt for all
religions. Lessing preaches tolerance in its noblest
aspect, tolerance born not of the rationalist's contempt, or the statesman's indifference, but rather

tolerance which is the genuine outcome of love and emu-
lation. Consequently, he makes his judge utter these
words:

> Now then, let each son strive with all his
> might to demonstrate his love devoid of
> selfishness. Let each one vie with his two
> brothers to bring to light the promised
> virtue of the ring he wears upon his finger.

Every religion—as Lessing here teaches—is to be
judged by its fruits rather than by its proofs. It
must be borne in mind, however, that the fruits are
not yet all garnered, nor will they be for a thousand
thousand years to come. The mystic appeal in religion
is here not overlooked by Lessing, as some critics
have charged, but it is undoubtedly subordinated to
the great end of producing good men on earth. The
wrangling brothers are admonished, each believing
that he has the genuine ring, to come to the aid of
its magic, not only with virtuous deeds and mere
morality, but—

> With the most fervent piety and devotion
> to his God.

Religion is therefore presented by Lessing as an instrument in the long education of the human race.

The relation of *Nathan the Wise* to Lessing's other
writings has been beautifully interpreted in a study
entitled *Lessing, Jesus and Kant* by Franz Horn. He
connects it with Lessing's *Education of the Human
Race*, the only work which he published after *Nathan*,
though he wrote various other things during 1779 and
1780. In this treatise he lays down certain principles, ideas, and axioms, "if there be any in things
like that". It contains his ideal of a religion, of
a new Gospel, which should as surely supersede the
New Testament as this superseded the Old. But how

and when is this ideal to be attained? It may be a
thousand thousand years before man will love virtue
for its own sake and do the good because it is the
good, not because it is to his advantage to do it.
The manner in which this ultimate and noble goal is
to be reached is proclaimed by Lessing in *Nathan* as
follows: "Judaism, Christianity, and Islam, the
three chief positive religions, differ in nonessen-
tials. Now each faith contains truth enough to make
man noble, true, and good, if he merely be willing to
subject it to the test of good deeds and of the love
of his neighbor." That is the gist of the Parable of
the Three Rings, the very heart of *Nathan the Wise*.
See the Appendix for a detailed account of the history of this famous parable.

    The two most important characters of the play are
found in the parable. The magnanimous Saladin was a
fixed figure of literary tradition, and Lessing took
him very much as he found him. Boccaccio's cunning
Jew Melchisedech became Lessing's wise *Nathan*, the
bearer of his message of love and good works, in fact,
his representative *humanus*. The plot is purely
romantic. Saladin is provided with a lost brother,
who had a son and a daughter by a German wife. The
girl appears in the play as Nathan's adopted daughter,
her brother as a hot-headed Templar, who falls in
love with the supposed Jewess. The end is a happy
family reunion, in which Mohammedans and Christians
embrace one another as kin, while the high-minded
Jew, who has brought it all about, receives the ac-
clamation and the benediction of all. There is no
real dramatic conflict anywhere, no clash of strong
wills. Once, to be sure, Nathan seems to be in danger from the machinations of the fanatical Patriarch
of Jerusalem, for whom the contemptible historical
Heraclius served as the prototype with here and
there, no doubt, a touch of bigotry suggested by
Goeze. But the Patriarch's malice turns out to be
only a passing threat; nothing comes of it, and the

peaceful drama moves on serenely to its happy ending.
But the "action" is never tame, for the lack of a
dramatic conflict is compensated by the superb skill
with which the characters are drawn.

The plot of *Nathan the Wise* has been most often
criticized on account of the awkwardness that Recha
and the Templar should turn out to be brother and
sister at the end of the drama, when they are in love
with each other. Among the characters, that of the
Dervish is perhaps the most improbable, even though
Lessing has portrayed him as an exceedingly clever
man. As in Boccaccio, Lessing also gives Saladin as
the Sultan before whom the story is told. That a
Nathan such as Lessing portrays really lived during
the Crusades is not at all likely, so scholars gener-
ally have concluded that the time and scene were evi-
dently suggested to Lessing by Boccaccio, Day 1,
Story 3 in the *Decameron*. It is still a frequently
repeated objection levelled by critics at Lessing
that the characters representing Christianity were
unfairly chosen if his aim was to represent Judaism,
Christianity, and Islam in their true light, unbiased
and impartially. But it must be borne in mind that
Lessing was writing for Christians, who believed in
the universality and undisputed superiority of their
faith. It was this bigotry, this intolerance, that
he wanted to shake, for in his view a belief in the
exclusive possession of the truth made man "at ease,
lazy, proud, and intolerant." Now Lessing does not
deny that the Mohammedan and the Jew are oftentimes
just as intolerant and bigoted as the Christian. Had
he written to improve these believers, he would, no
doubt, have made Nathan a Christian. Consequently,
he made Saladin better than history makes him, and
Nathan was presented as a Jew, not a Christian. No
one will deny the truth of Nathan's character as a
Jew unless he believes in the truth of Marlow's *Jew
of Malta*, particularly if he recalls that Jesus was a
Jew and that Lessing's bosom-friend, the kindly Moses

Mendelssohn was a Jew. The Jews were the unjustly
injured and despised party, which was another good
reason why a man like Lessing should side with them,
just as he had taken their part years before in his
play *The Jews*. Every Christian reader would readily
own that Christianity could produce a Nathan, in fact,
any number of them, but he had first to be taught that
Judaism could also produce such a man. Daja and the
Templar are very natural Christians, and Lessing's
Patriarch is considerably better than the actual
patriarch of the time, the base and despicable
Auvergnac Heraclius.

In spite of any faults or weaknesses that have been
levelled against *Nathan*, no one will deny that its
setting is excellent, considering the purpose which
Lessing had in mind. Moreover, it is brimming over
with charity, with pathos, and with humor. The whole
drama leaves with the reader a strong impression of
the essential goodness of humanity. It seems to
imply that in spite of superficial faults in the
makeup and actions of human beings the hearts of men
and women are sound. An atmosphere of sunniness and
good cheer pervades the whole play which intensifies
the idealistic teaching that it conveys.

Much has been written concerning the merits, the
character, and even the aim of Lessing's *Nathan the
Wise*. Some well-meaning critics have even tried to
override Lessing's own estimate of his powers, laid
down in the well-known self-confession in his *Hamburg
Dramaturgy*, and have made him out to be a born poet
like Shakespeare and Goethe. In the same fashion they
have likewise tried to set aside Lessing's own estimate of his own brain-child *Nathan the Wise*. He calls
it a "dramatic poem, which would read well," but he is
doubtful whether it can be produced on the stage. But
the German poet Platen later calls it a *tragedy* in the
lines:

German tragedies I have read by the dozens,
    the best one
Seemed this one to me, although without
    spectres and spooks.

A French translator has, in fact, even gone so far as
to call it a *comedy*. The title of Cubières de
Palmézeaux' French translation of *Nathan the Wise*
reads: *Nathan le Sage, ou le Juif Philosophe*, comédie
héroïque. It is of course not a *comedy*, and it is
certainly no *tragedy*. James Russell Lowell has described it as an "essay on toleration in the form of
a dialogue," which comes close to Lessing's own estimate of his *Nathan*, even though it may sound somewhat
cold and unappreciative. To try to make the play a
comedy, as Cubières de Palmézeaux apparently did, or
a *tragedy*, as Platen would have it, is to make of it
what Lessing did not mean it to be, and what he himself knew it was not. It is not detracting from the
merits of the work or of the dramatist in any way to
give it its right name and place, namely, *a dramatic
poem*. Lessing was too much the *true artist* who, in
his own words, "would ten times rather let undeserved
blame rest upon himself than undeserved praise."
Lessing's *Nathan* is his best known work in general
literature, and this high regard is due less to its
excellence as a drama than to the charmingly told
ring-parable, the beautiful and ideal character of
Nathan, and the noble aim of Lessing himself. Take
any play in the classical period of German literature
and you will find that there are none so well con-
structed as Lessing's three masterpieces, *Minna von
Barnhelm, Emilia Galotti,* and *Nathan the Wise*. In
spite of Lessing's doubts about the suitability of
Nathan as a stage-play, no plays are better adapted
for the stage than Lessing's three, just as they
stand written, and none are less in need of summaries
of acts and scenes or of a running commentary. It
must be concluded that this excellence is due to
Lessing's master craftsmanship in the drama and to
his great critical genius.

The eighteenth century is known as the Age of Enlightenment or the Age of Reason, as the French call it, and its literature was strongly influenced by the liberal thought of the time. Swift's *Tale of a Tub* had been directed against creeds and Voltaire's *Mahomet* against fanaticism. In his drama *Les Guèbres* Voltaire had also pleaded for religious toleration. Lessing had therefore found suggestions for his *Nathan the Wise* in the existing literature as well as in the controversies of his own intellectual life in Germany. But critics agree unanimously that *Nathan* expresses the best thought of the Age of Enlightenment on the subject of religion. Although the actual writing of this work required only a few months, its substance of doctrine had matured slowly in Lessing's mind over many years. *Nathan* has consequently depths and far-reaching implications which make it one of the most fascinating of all dramas which have a specific religious tendency. In it Lessing hewed a pathway, as it were, between extreme orthodoxy on the one hand and extreme rationalism on the other. His thesis is, in effect, that all religions are provisionally true insofar as they make for goodness in human relations. How sorely good human relations are still lacking in our twentieth century must be obvious to every thinking man and, lest we forget, in 1979 *Nathan the Wise* will be two-hundred years old!

Lessing has treated his great theme nobly and sympathetically, like a clairvoyant who knows that he is creating a literary masterpiece which will occupy the minds of men for centuries to come. The lack of violent dramatic conflict levelled as a criticism against *Nathan* fades into insignificance before the greater universal conflict which Lessing clarified so beautifully. Here lies his greatness as "the great enlightener", the great humanitarian. His message, which was far ahead of his age, has—unfortunately—not been heeded! What a beautiful world it might have been, if only Lessing's message in *Nathan the Wise* had been heeded!

Nathan was first played at Berlin in 1783, but it
was performed so poorly that the house was empty at
the third production. Since Goethe and Schiller
brought it out later in the eighteenth century at
Weimar with Iffland in the lead-role of Nathan, the
play has held its place on the German stage. It has
always required a first-class actor, such as Iffland,
Schroeder, Devrient, or Seydelmann, to make *Nathan the
Wise* a success. It has been stated above that there
is no strong dramatic conflict in *Nathan*. It was for
this reason that Lessing hesitated to call it a *drama*;
instead, he gave it a metrical form and called it
rather a *dramatic poem*. Although *Nathan* cannot correctly be called a *drama* in the strictest technical
sense, and certainly neither a comedy nor a tragedy,
Lessing was, nevertheless, an innovator of great sig-
nificance in this work. In his choice of blank verse
for *Nathan the Wise* he was virtually—but not in the
strictest sense—a pioneer. It had become quite
obvious to all progressive minds that the alexandrine,
which had held sway in all serious drama for more than
a century in Germany, was all wrong. It was ill
adapted to the genius of the German language, and especially ill adapted, with its rigid structure and
its monotonous cadence, to brisk or impassioned dialogue. The question was what could be used in its
place. The increasing vogue of Shakespeare in Germany
opened the eyes of some German scholars to the pos-
sibilities of blank verse, which seemed to offer an
answer to the problem. In his *Fragments* Herder came
out strongly in favor of blank verse as the form that
would combine strength with freedom. It was this form
which Lessing chose for his *Nathan*, a form which was
admirably suited for his trenchant dialectic.

Nathan the Wise thus became the first prominent
classical play in Germany written in blank verse, and
from that time on it became the standard form for the
poetic dramas of Goethe, Schiller and later Grill-
parzer. Lessing himself was quite aware that his

blank verse was not faultless. James Russell Lowell,
commenting on Lessing's verse, states that Lessing's
prose can leap and run but that his verse is always
thinking of its feet. He frequently repeats a word,
merely to make out the proper number of syllables. It
is the writer's opinion that Lessing's blank verse is
at its best in the Parable of the Three Rings. In
fact, Lessing himself readily admitted that he could
write better prose than verse. Indeed, those critics
who have most severely criticized his verse have
often laid too much stress on Lessing's own remark
that the verses in *Nathan* would be "much worse, if
they were better." All that he meant to say in these
words was that his verses were good enough for his
purpose; if he had spent more time and labor on them,
the play might have suffered in other ways, for instance, in the clearness of its style and the spirit
of its dialogue. But the truth of the matter is this,
and it cannot be denied: the blank verse in Lessing's
Nathan is poor in the elements of poetry; it does not
glow, nor does it flow. On the positive side, however, no one can deny that it talks admirably. The
line as a rhythmic unit does not count for much.
Lessing breaks it up in various ways. He is lavish
in his use of *enjambement* and frequently pays little
attention to the iambic cadence. His nervous, inci-
sive style, with its frequent cacophonies, is certainly very different from the smooth and soulful verse-
melody of Goethe or the rhythmic sonorousness of
Schiller. But in spite of these faults, to Lessing
goes the honor of inaugurating blank verse into German
drama, and it was this metrical form which was adopted
from that time onward as the standard type in German
verse drama.

The scene of *Nathan the Wise* is laid in Jerusalem
during the twelfth century, the period of the crusades.
The play is not an historical chronicle, however, but
rather a problem play or a drama of purpose. At
Jerusalem, Jew, Christian, and Mohammedan meet. For

many centuries they have been meeting there with jeal-
ousy and religious enmity in their hearts. In the
twelfth century, toleration was a rare thing. Saladin
actually protected the Jews, but he tore down many a
cross and destroyed many a Christian religious article
when he conquered Jerusalem. The real scene of *Nathan*,
however, is the eighteenth century rather than the
colorful twelfth century of the crusades. This so-
called Age of Enlightenment ultimately touched com-
paratively few in the German States, in fact, in most
European states. It was, to be sure an age of benevo-
lent despots—Frederick the Great, Maria Theresa,
Catherine the Great—but hardly of general freedom.
The motto was "everything for the people, but nothing
by the people." Consequently in his *Nathan the Wise*
Lessing spoke primarily to his own intolerant and
superstitious compatriots, and as his hero he chose
his Jewish friend, Moses Mendelssohn, whom he had met
over a chessboard in Berlin in 1754.

It is fitting to close this discussion with Goethe's
high appreciation of the mission of Lessing's *Nathan
the Wise* as a play, in the following words:

> May the well-known story of the rings, so
> happily presented, ever remind the German
> public that it is not called merely to see,
> but also to hear and thoughtfully consider.
> At the same time, may the divine feeling of
> toleration and forbearance which permeates
> it remain sacred and dear to the nation.

The translation here presented has dispensed with
Lessing's blank verse, and prose has been used instead.
Other than that deviation, a sincere attempt has been
made to keep as close as possible to Lessing's text
and especially to Lessing's spirit.

Walter Frank Charles Ade

Munster, Indiana,
June, 1972

CHRONOLOGY

(Lessing: born, Saxony, 1729; died, Brunswick, 1781)

Title

1747	*Damon, oder die wahre Freundschaft* (Lustspiel)
1748	*Der junge Gelehrte in der Einbildung* (Lustspiel)
1748	*Der Misogyne* (Lustspiel)
1749	*Die alte Jungfer* (Lustspiel)
1749	*Die Juden*
1749	*Der Freigeist*
1749–1750	*Beiträge zur Historie und Aufnahme des Theaters*
1750	*Der Schatz* (Lustspiel)
1750	*Palaion*
1751	*Kleinigkeiten*
1751	*Simon Lemnius*
1751	*Das Neueste aus dem Reiche des Witzes*
1752	*Des Herrn von Voltaire kleinere historische Schriften*
1753	*Das Christentum der Vernunft*
1753	*Vade mecum für Lange*
1754	*Rettungen des Horaz*
1754	*Vermischte Schriften des Herrn Christlob Mylius*
1754–1758	*Theatralische Bibliothek*
1754–1758	*Giangir, oder der verschmähte Thron* (Fragment)
1754–1758	*Samuel Henzi* (Fragment)
1755	*Miss Sara Sampson* (bürgerliches Trauerspiel)
1755	*Pope ein Metaphysiker* (mit Moses Mendelssohn)
1756	*Die glückliche Erbin* (nach Goldoni)

1756   *Briefwechsel mit Nicolai und Moses Mendelssohn*
        über die Tragödie
1757   *Das befreite Rom* (Fragment)
1758   *Codrus* (Fragment)
1758   *Kleonnis* (Fragment)
1758   *Philotas* (Trauerspiel; Einakter)
1758   *Das Horoskop* (Fragment)
1758   *Doktor Faust* (Fragment)
1758   *Leben des Sophokles*
1759   *Fabeln, 3 Bücher, nebst Abhandlungen über*
        diese Dichtungsart
1759   *Friedrichs von Logau Sinngedichte*
1759–   *Briefe die neueste Literatur betreffend*
1764
1760   *Das Theater des Herrn Diderot* (Übersetzung)
1760–   *Fatima* (Fragment)
1765
1760–   *Alcibiades in Persien* (Fragment)
1765
1760–   *Nero* (Fragment)
1765
1760–   *Philoktet* (Fragment)
1765
1760–   *Die Witzlinge* (Lustspiel)(Fragment)
1765
1766   *Laokoön*
1767   *Minna von Barnhelm* (Lustspiel)
1767–   *Hamburgische Dramaturgie*
1769
1768–   *Briefe antiquarischen Inhalts*
1769
1769   *Kleinigkeiten* (Gedichte)
1769   *Wie die Alten den Tod gebildet* (Aufsatz)
1770   *Berengarius Turonensis*
1772   *Emilia Galotti* (Trauerspiel)
1773–   *Zur Geschichte und Literatur* (3 Bände)
1781
1774–   *Fragmente des Wolfenbüttel'schen Ungenannten*
1778   (Raimarus' Apologie oder Schutzschrift für
            die vernünftigen Verehrer Gottes)

1777   *Über den Beweis des Geistes und der Kraft*
1777   *Das Testament Johannis*
1778   *Eine Duplik*
1778   *Eine Parabel*
1778   *Axiomata*
1778   *Anti-Goeze*
1778-   *Ernst und Falk* (Gespräche für Freimäurer)
1780
1779   *Nathan der Weise* (dramatisches Gedicht)
1780   *Die Erziehung des Menschengeschlechts*

DRAMATIS PERSONAE[1]

SULTAN SALADIN[2]
SITTAH, his sister
NATHAN, a rich Jew of Jerusalem
RECHA, his adopted daughter
DAJA, a Christian woman living in
      Nathan's house as Recha's companion
A young KNIGHT TEMPLAR[3]
A DERVISH[4]
The PATRIARCH OF JERUSALEM[5]
A FRIAR
An EMIR[6] and several MAMELUKES[7] in
      Saladin's service

The scene is in Jerusalem

---

[1] The drama is set in the time of the crusades.

[2] Sultan Saladin was one of the most successful defenders of Palestine.

[3] The Knights Templars, also known simply as Templars or as Poor Knights of the Temple, were members of an order, which was both religious and military, founded at Jerusalem in the twelfth century to protect Christian pilgrims and the Holy Sepulchre.

[4] A dervish was a member of a Mohammedan order sworn to poverty and to celibacy.

[5] The Patriarch of Jerusalem was the high Christian church authority and possessed more than ordinary episcopal dignity and power.

[6] The Emirs were Mohammedan chieftains and descendants of Mohammed.

[7] The Mamelukes were members of a warrior class, who were originally slaves.

NATHAN THE WISE

"Introite, nam et heic Dii sunt."[1]

ACT ONE

Scene i

[The entrance hall of Nathan's house. Nathan is returning from a journey. Daja comes running up to
meet him.]

DAJA. Is it really you? O, Nathan! Thank God
you've now come back to us at last!

NATHAN. Yes, Daja, thank God. But tell me, what
makes you say "at last"? Was it my plan to come home
earlier? Or, if I'd planned or wished it, could I
possibly have done so? From Babylon to Jerusalem is
a good two hundred leagues as I was forced to travel,
detouring now right, now left, from the main highway.
And collecting debts isn't exactly an easy chore
either, you know.

DAJA. O, Nathan, how wretched you might have
been! Your house —

NATHAN. Caught fire. Yes, I've heard that news
already. God grant that now I've learned the whole
of my misfortune!

DAJA. It might have burned down to the very
ground.

---

[1]"Enter, for here too there are gods."

NATHAN. Why, then we'd simply build a new and better one.

DAJA. Quite right, but Recha came within an inch of being burned to death as well.

NATHAN. Burned, you say? My Recha? That I wasn't told. O, then I'd have no need of any house! She came within an inch, you say, of being burned to death? Nearly burned to death! Or was she really burned to death? Come, out with it, tell me the truth! Don't torture me like this. Tell me this minute — she has been burned to death! — and kill me on the spot.

DAJA. If she'd been burned to death, you'd surely not expect to hear it from my lips.

NATHAN. Why scare me then? O, Recha, O, my Recha!

DAJA. Your Recha? But is she really yours?

NATHAN. You may be sure that day will never dawn when I'll stop calling this dear child my own.

DAJA. And do you call all that you have your own without a better title to it?

NATHAN. I've no clearer title to anything I own. All else that's mine was given to me by Fortune or by Nature. This dear child is the only gift I owe to Virtue.

DAJA. O, Nathan, how dearly must I pay for all your goodness! If the name of goodness can indeed apply to your motive concerning Recha.

NATHAN. My motive concerning Recha? What *do* you mean with that remark?

DAJA. My conscience —

NATHAN. First, Daja, let me tell you —

DAJA. I'm telling you, my conscience —

NATHAN. — what a gorgeous cloth I've bought for
you in Babylon! It is so rare, so very precious!
The cloth I bring for Recha is scarcely any better
than what I've bought for you.

DAJA. O, what does that matter? I'm telling
you my conscience won't be silent any longer.

NATHAN. And how you'll love the bracelets, ear-
rings, finger-rings and golden chains I've picked up
for you in Damascus! I can't wait to see your joy!

DAJA. Now isn't that just like you! Is that all
you have to say? Must you be always giving, giving?

NATHAN. Please take my gifts as gladly as I give
them. Not another word!

DAJA. Not another word! Who can doubt, dear
Nathan, that you're the soul of honor and generosity
itself? And yet —

NATHAN. I'm only a Jew. That's what you mean, I
suppose.

DAJA. Surely, Nathan, you know much better what
I mean!

NATHAN. Well, then, why not be silent?

DAJA. Yes, I'll be silent, but if any sin results
from this in the sight of God, a sin I cannot hinder,
well, then, that sin's not mine. It's yours and yours
alone.

NATHAN. Yes, yes, let it be mine alone. But
where is Recha now? Where does she stay so long? Are
you by any chance deceiving me? And tell me, does she
know that I've come home?

DAJA. Perhaps you can answer that. Every fibre
in her body trembles with terror. Her fancy colors
all her thoughts with fire. In sleep her troubled
mind starts up in fright, awake she's in a trance.
One moment she's less than human, the next she seems
more like an angel.

NATHAN. O, my poor child! How frail we humans
are!

DAJA. This morning for a long while she lay in
bed with closed eyes as if she were dead. Then suddenly she started from her couch and shouted: "Listen! Listen! My father's camels draw near! Don't
you hear them? I hear his gentle voice again." But
then her eyes grew dim and soon her head slid off her
arm on which it was supported and fell back again in
slumber on her pillow. I hastened to the gate and
saw that she was right, that you'd really come home
to us at long last. It wasn't any wonder though, for
since you left, her whole soul's been with you only —
and with him.

NATHAN. With *him*? What *him*?

DAJA. The man who saved her from the fire.

NATHAN. And who was that? Where is he now? Who
was the man who saved my darling Recha?

DAJA. It was a young Knight Templar, brought
here shortly before a prisoner, and pardoned by Sultan
Saladin himself.

NATHAN. This Templar's life was spared by
Saladin? Could any greater miracle have saved my
Recha's life? O, my God!

DAJA. If he'd not boldly risked his life again —
the life spared by the grace of Saladin himself! —
no doubt our darling Recha would have perished in the
flames.

NATHAN. Where is he, Daja, where is this noble
hero now? Tell me, Daja, please, where is he, and
lead me quickly to his feet. Whatever treasures I've
left at home with you, I'm sure you've given him already and promised him much more.

DAJA. There was no time to do that, Nathan, none
at all.

NATHAN. Don't tell me you've not given him anything.

DAJA. He wouldn't let me, Nathan, he wouldn't let
me! No one knows where he comes from, nor where he's
gone. He didn't know our house, but fearless —
guided only by his ear — he plunged through smoke and
fire. Holding his mantle before him as a shield, on,
on, he went until he reached the spot where he heard
piercing screams for help. We'd already given him up
for lost, when all at once, bursting through the
flames, he stood before us bearing the helpless Recha
in his arms. Then, deaf to our sobbing thanks, he
gently set her down and disappeared among the crowd.

NATHAN. I hope he hasn't disappeared forever.

DAJA. A few days later, we saw him once again
strolling among the palms that shade the Holy Sepulchre. Delighted that I'd found him, I went to him and

thanked him once again. I begged him then most earnestly to come with me and see the grateful girl who
could not rest till she had wept her thanks out at
his feet.

NATHAN. Well, what happened then?

DAJA. It was all in vain. He turned a deaf ear
to my pleading and heaped such bitter scorn on me —

NATHAN. That you were frightened and stayed
away.

DAJA. Not at all! On the contrary, I went to
him again day after day to crave a visit to the grateful Recha. But every day he merely scoffed at me.
I've taken many insults from this man and I'd have
gladly suffered more. But then he stopped his walks
among the palms that shade the Holy Sepulchre. He's
gone away and no one knows where he can now be found.
Why so amazed, Nathan? What are you wondering?

NATHAN. I'm wondering what effect this insult
must have on Recha's mind. To be despised by that
very person whom she must always highly honor! To be
attracted to this man and at the same time be re-
pulsed by him! Her head and heart must surely be at
odds struggling to decide if anger or if sorrow should
prevail. Then, Fancy, entering this inner struggle,
creates the dreamer. First the head must play the
heart, and then the heart must play the head! This is
indeed a sad exchange! But if I know my Recha well,
she'll choose the heart. She dreams, you say?

DAJA. Yes, but her dreams are sweet and very
beautiful.

NATHAN. But nevertheless her dreams have got the
upper hand!

DAJA. One whim she seems to cling to most, one
that means much to her. She's convinced her Templar's
not a human being and serves no mortal man. She
thinks an angel whom she's trusted from her childhood
on stepped from his dwelling in a cloud and — as a
Templar — came floating through the fire to rescue
her. O, Nathan, please, don't smile! Who knows? If
you must smile, at least permit your Recha to indulge
that fancy which Christian, Jew and Mussulman all
share alike. Her dreaming is so sweet!

NATHAN. I like it too. But go, dear Daja, go!
See how she is. See if she's well enough now for me
to speak to her. Then I'll go out to seek that wilful
and eccentric guardian angel of hers and — if he's
still inclined to live among us mortals here on earth
and play the boorish knight — why, then you may be
sure I'll find him and bring him here to us.

DAJA. The task you're undertaking isn't easy.

NATHAN. You can rely on me, dear Daja! Then will
sweet dreams yield to a sweeter truth, for after all
is said and done to a human heart a man is far more
dear than an angel. You'll not be angry with me, will
you, Daja, if by this means our angel-dreamer's fully
cured?

DAJA. O, Nathan, how good you are and yet so
wicked! I'm going to Recha now. No, I won't either,
for, if you'll look over there, you'll see that here
she comes herself!

Scene ii

[RECHA, NATHAN, and DAJA]

RECHA. O, father, is it really you in person?
Are you really home again safe and sound? I thought
you'd merely sent your voice ahead of you. Where are
you lingering still? What mountains, streams and
deserts still part us now? Here we are, so close together again, face to face, and yet you do not hasten
to fold your Recha in your arms? Poor Recha! In your
absence she was almost burned alive! Yes *almost* —
almost burned to death! But, please, don't shudder.
It's such a terrible death to die by fire.

NATHAN. My child, my darling child!

RECHA. You had to cross the Euphrates, the
Tigris, and the Jordan — who knows what other waters?
If only you knew how often I've trembled in fear for
your safety, before the fire came so close to me! And,
since that narrow escape from my inferno, I've come to
think that death by water would be so refreshing, so
comforting and soothing. But then you didn't drown,
nor did I die by fire. For that great mercy let's re-
joice and lift our hearts to God. He guided both your
ship and you on the wings of His *invisible* angel-host
across the treacherous rivers. He also beckoned to *my*
good angel to bear me through the fire on his white
wings — but *visibly*.

NATHAN. (Aside) His white wings? Yes, yes, I
understand. She means the Templar's broad white cloak
spread out wide before him as he came to save her.

RECHA. *Visibly*, Nathan, *visibly*, I tell you. God
sent my guardian angel *visibly* to bear me through the
searing flames, covered safely by his wings. And so

I've seen my angel face to face — *my own, my own* good
angel!

NATHAN. No doubt my Recha's worthy of an angel!
You'd see in him, I know, nothing more beautiful than
he'd be sure to see in you.

RECHA. (Smiling) O, father, who are you really
flattering — the angel, or yourself?

NATHAN. Any man, my dear. Yes, any *human* man,
such as is born on any given day, who'd saved your
life as he's just done, must necessarily appear to be
an angel in your sight. It's only natural that he
must and should.

RECHA. No, no, Nathan, that's not at all the kind
of angel that I mean! Oh, no, I mean a genuine angel,
not a human one. And don't forget, dear Nathan, that
you yourself have taught me it's quite possible that
angels do exist and may be seen. You've told me so
yourself, God works great wonders to help those who
love Him. And you, Nathan, you must surely know how
fervently I love Him!

NATHAN. I'm sure of that and also that He loves
you. For you and such as you, my darling, He hourly
works His wonders, and He's done precisely that from
all eternity.

RECHA. That's how I love to hear you speak.

NATHAN. I wonder why? It sounds so natural, so
commonplace. Suppose, for instance, that a Templar —
a mere human, not an angel — had saved you from the
fire. Tell me, dear Recha, would you think it less a
miracle because of that? The real wonder, as I see
it, is that true miracles become so commonplace, such

everyday occurrences in our lives. Without this universal miracle, could thinking men use the word so
childishly, like children gaping at whatever they find
strange and think the newest things are always the
most wonderful?

DAJA. (To Nathan) Do you want to tax still more
or even break her overwrought brain with these subtle
arguments?

NATHAN. Daja, listen to me! Isn't it a great
enough miracle to find my dearest Recha saved by one
who himself had first to be saved by no less a miracle? And, take it from me, it was no minor miracle
which made it possible for him to carry out this dar-
ing deed. Tell me, I ask you, who ever heard before
this time that Saladin had spared a Templar's life?
Who ever heard that such a knight could dare hope
Saladin would spare him, or for his ransom could offer more than his swordbelt or at most his sword?

RECHA. But, father, don't you see, your words
are clear proof for me that it couldn't be a Templar
in the flesh, but merely the likeness of one. If, as
you state, no captive Templar ever before came to
Jerusalem except to certain death, and if no man of
his Order was ever previously granted freedom to walk
the streets of our fair city, explain, I beg you, how
could a Templar suddenly loom up at midnight and rescue me from death?

NATHAN. Well, look at that! She argues very
well. Daja, you answer her. You've told me he came
here a prisoner, so likely you know more.

DAJA. Well, yes, I know what people say. Rumor
has it that the only reason why stern Saladin showed
such great mercy to this man was due entirely to his

strange resemblance to a younger brother whom Saladin
had dearly loved. But since already more than twenty
years have passed since the child in question died —
whose name's not known nor where he lived — the rumor
seems an idle tale and certainly incredible, to say
the least.

NATHAN. No, no, dear Daja, why should it seem incredible? Can it be that you've rejected it because
of wishful thinking, merely to make room for things
less credible, as is so often the case? It's a well-
known fact, you know, that Saladin dearly loves his
race. Why, then, shouldn't Saladin have had a younger
brother who was his favorite when still a child? Tell
me, have two people never looked alike? Do you suppose an old love can't return again? And don't the
same causes produce the same effects? Since when is
that not so? I fail to see what's so incredible here.
And if it were incredible, my wise Daja, why then it
wouldn't be a miracle any more. Or is it perhaps
that only *your* miracles, dear lady, demand, or shall I
say deserve, belief?

DAJA. O, Nathan, now you're making fun of me.

NATHAN. Well, you mocked at me first. But none-
the-less, dear Recha, your intrepid rescue remains a
miracle just the same! It was indeed a miracle, made
possible only by Him who by weak threads can turn in
sport, if not in mockery, the stern laws and deep-laid
plans of sultans!

RECHA. O, my dear father, if I'm wrong, you know
that I'm wrong only because of my ignorance, nothing
else.

NATHAN. I do, my dear, and what I like still more
is that you want to learn. But pay attention now! A

brow molded this way or arched that way; a nose shaped
thus or thus; eyebrows full or delicately pencilled,
resting on a ridge now blunt, now sharp; a line, a
bend, a fold, an angle, or a mole; or other more dis-
tinctive features on the face of some Frankish European man, and you are rescued from the fire — in
Asia! If that's no wonder, my miracle-hungry ladies,
why trouble an angel?

DAJA. O, come, Nathan -- if I may say so, what
harm can there possibly be, after all, to want an
angel as her rescuer rather than a man of flesh and
blood? By doing so, she feels drawn much more closely to the primary, the mysterious cause of her salvation.

NATHAN. Why, that's pride, mere pride! Silver
tongs, you know, are favored by the iron pot to draw
it from the furnace, so it may dream that it's a
costly silver vase. You're asking me what harm
there's in it? Well, then I'll ask what good it does?
As you express it, it's to feel that God is so much
nearer. This thought of yours — why, it's pure
folly, if — indeed — not blasphemy. It's harmful
and brings turmoil to the soul. But, please, I ask
you, listen for a moment. Whether the being who rescued you be thought of as an angel or a mere man,
wouldn't you gladly repay in every possible way his
magnificent deed, for having risked his life to rescue yours? Well, now, suppose he were an angel. What
possible repayment could you make to him in that event
for his great deed? "I'll thank him," you'll most
likely say, "I'll sigh to him and pray; I'll melt in
grateful tears before his feet; I'll fast, give alms,
and celebrate his festive saint!" All that amounts
to nothing! How so, you ask? Well, it seems to me,
by acting this way, you and your good neighbors gain
much more than he. All your fasting won't make him

grow fat, your charities for him won't make him rich.
Nor will your worship add anything to his glory, nor
your great faith in him make him a mightier angel.
Isn't that so? But suppose a human being — not an
angel — were involved, what then?

    DAJA. I'm well aware that a human being's needs
would give us much more opportunity to serve him. And
Heaven only knows, we wished to do just that! But
this man neither wants nor needs a single thing! He's
happy with his lot, at peace with himself, as only
angels are or can be.

    RECHA. And now, when he's vanished ...

    NATHAN. Vanished? What do you mean by *vanished*?
Do you mean by chance that he's no longer to be seen
beneath the palms? If that's your meaning, tell me,
didn't you search for him in any other places?

    DAJA. No, we didn't! Why should we?

    NATHAN. No, Daja, no, you didn't, naturally! But
this neglect may cause you grief! Suppose, my pretty
dreamers, your angel should be sick!

    RECHA. Sick!

    DAJA. Sick! O, don't say that!

    RECHA. How my heart shudders at the thought!
Feel my cold brow, Daja! One moment it's fever-hot,
now suddenly it's icy cold!

    NATHAN. This man's a Frank, a European, you know,
a stranger here. He's young, not used to hunger and
to vigil, nor to the heavy tasks assigned to him just
now.

RECHA. Sick!

DAJA. Nathan's only supposing, dear Recha.

NATHAN. What a plight! Just think, there he lies
alone. He's sick, without a friend or gold to buy
friends for him.

RECHA. O, father, please, my heart!

NATHAN. No care, no good advice, no friendly sympathy! A victim of pain — perhaps even of death —
he now lies ill!

RECHA. Where? Please, Nathan, tell me *where*?

NATHAN. This man who for a fellow human being —
one he'd never seen before — leaped in the fire ...

DAJA. O, Nathan, please have mercy! Spare her,
please, I beg you!

NATHAN. Who wouldn't come here again to get to
know better the person he'd so gallantly rescued from
the flames, merely to spare himself your gratitude.

DAJA. Please, please, have pity on her, Nathan!

NATHAN. Who doesn't even wish to see her any
more, unless it be to save her again, a fellow human
being! But no more of this! It was enough for him,
you see, that she was human!

DAJA. Nathan, I'm begging you to stop! Just look
at her!

NATHAN. He's on his death-bed now and confort-
less, except for the memory of his gallant deed

rescuing a human being from her death.

DAJA. I beg you, Nathan, stop this torture! Don't
you see, you're killing her!

NATHAN. He's the one you've killed or might have
killed. Recha, O my dear Recha! This is medicine —
not poison — that I'm bringing you. Come be yourself again! Your Templar is alive and is perhaps not
even sick!

RECHA. Is that the truth? Are you saying he's
not dead, not even sick?

NATHAN. He's certainly not dead, I'm sure of
that! For God rewards good deeds, rewards them even
here below on earth. But surely, Recha, I needn't
teach you what you know already. How much easier it
is to dream our pious dreams than to act bravely! A
worthless man will often dream fine dreams merely to
escape a humane task, though it may sometimes be his
motive's hidden from himself.

RECHA. O, father, never leave your Recha alone
and to herself again! Isn't it quite possible that
he's only gone on a little journey?

NATHAN. Yes, Recha, no doubt that's it. But down
below I see a Mussulman looking over my camels and
their load with a curious eye. Who is that man? Tell
me, Daja, do you know him?

DAJA. Yes, of course, I know him. It's your dervish.

NATHAN. Who?

DAJA. Why, your chess-companion — your dervish!

NATHAN. Al-Hafi! My friend Al-Hafi?

DAJA. He's the Sultan's treasurer now.

NATHAN. Al-Hafi? You must be dreaming! No,
you're right, there he is! He's here in person! He's
coming here to me — go quickly in the house! And now
I wonder what I'll hear?

Scene iii

[NATHAN and the DERVISH]

DERVISH. Don't be so startled, Nathan! Open your
eyes wide and wonder!

NATHAN. I'm still not certain if it's really you.
You a dervish and dressed in silks?

DERVISH. Well, why not, Nathan, why not? Can nothing good come of a dervish, nothing good at all?
Please tell me why, if that's a fact.

NATHAN. I've no doubt at all a dervish can amount
to much, if he sets his mind to do so. But I've always thought somehow that a dervish tried and true
would — come what may — refuse to be anything other
than a dervish.

DERVISH. Why, by the Prophet, perhaps it's true
that I'm no genuine dervish, but when one must ...

NATHAN. What's this I hear? *Must* — a dervish
must? No man should live by *must,* and certainly not a
dervish. What *must* one?

DERVISH. What an honest man would have him do,
and he's convinced is right. That *must* a dervish do!

NATHAN. By Heaven, what you say is true. Come
here, good fellow, let me now embrace you. You're
still, I hope, my friend.

DERVISH. Of course, Nathan, of course, but don't
you want to know first what I've now become?

NATHAN. No. I'll take my chance, in spite of
what they've made of you!

DERVISH. It's possible, you know, my position in
the State may now be such that my friendship might
prove to be embarrassing, even burdensome, to you.

NATHAN. If in your heart you're still a dervish,
why then I'll trust both it and you. Your office in
the State — as far as I'm concerned — in that case
is a cloak and nothing more.

DERVISH. Which none-the-less must still be kept
in mind! Or don't you think so? But now please tell
me, at your own court what should I be?

NATHAN. A dervish, pure and simple, nothing more,
and — very possibly — my cook.

DERVISH. Oh, really! So in your service you'd
make me unlearn my present trade? Your cook!
Couldn't you make me your butler too? You'll confess, I'm sure, that Saladin knows me better. He's
made me his treasurer, I'll have you know!

NATHAN. You? His treasurer?

DERVISH. His smaller treasure, the treasure of

his household, you must understand, of course. His
greater treasure's still managed by his father.

NATHAN. His household's very big!

DERVISH. It's bigger than you think, for every
beggar's a member of it too.

NATHAN. But it's a well-known fact that Saladin
hates the beggar horde.

DERVISH. So much so, that he'd like nothing better than blot them out completely. But in attempting
that, he may himself become a beggar.

NATHAN. Well done, good Saladin, bravo! That's
exactly what I mean!

DERVISH. Actually he's a beggar now, although not
known as one. Every sunset sees his treasury emptier
than empty. However high the morning's tide may be,
the ebb-tide comes before each noon's at hand.

NATHAN. Drained by canals he can neither fill nor
close.

DERVISH. You've hit the nail right on the head.

NATHAN. I know I have.

DERVISH. It's certainly an evil hour when princes
are the vultures among carcases, but ten times worse
when they themselves are the carcases among vultures.

NATHAN. It's not as bad as that, good dervish,
surely it's not as bad as that!

DERVISH. Talk's cheap, Nathan. Well, now what's
your offer to take my place?

NATHAN. What does your office pay?

DERVISH. Pay *me*? Not much, I fear. But for *you*,
Nathan, it could be very profitable indeed. For when
the treasury's at ebb-tide — as often is the case —
why then you'd simply open up your flood-gates, advance the needed money, and charge as high an interest
as you please!

NATHAN. With interest compounded on the interest,
I assume.

DERVISH. That's exactly what I mean.

NATHAN. Until my capital's merely interest, nothing more.

DERVISH. Now tell me, Nathan, doesn't that tempt
you? If that's the case, why then we'll have to part.
That's all that's left for us and our past friendship!
For I must tell you, Nathan, I counted very much on
you.

NATHAN. Did you really? Counted on me? How did
you count on me?

DERVISH. I hoped you'd help me carry out the duties
of my office honorably, by offering me an ever-open
treasury. Why do you shake your head?

NATHAN. Well now, let's understand each other,
my good friend. There's a distinction here, you know.
You, my friend, are you. Al-Hafi, as a dervish, has
my fullest welcome, but Al-Hafi, as Saladin's officer,
that's quite a different matter. To him ...

DERVISH. I thought as much! You'd gladly help
your friend. You'd be kind if prudence would permit
it. As always, you'd be prudent, but at the same
time wise. But, please, be patient and hear me out.
You're splitting one Al-Hafi into two, but it could
well be these two will separate of their own accord.
This silken robe of honor which I'm wearing now was
given to me by Saladin. Look at it well before it
fades and turns to rags, rags fit to clothe a dervish. Soon this costly robe'll hang on a nail in old
Jerusalem, and I'll be found again beside the Ganges.
There barefoot with my teachers I'll be strolling at
my leisure on its hot sand.

NATHAN. Well, that's precisely what I'd expect
you'd do! You mean you'll be yourself again.

DERVISH. And play chess with them.

NATHAN. I know that is your greatest joy!

DERVISH. What do you suppose seduced me? Surely
you don't think I'd be no more a beggar or that I'd
ever want to play the rich man among my fellow-beg-
gars? Surely, Nathan, you don't believe that in a
moment's time I'd change the richest beggar into the
poorest rich man?

NATHAN. No, no, my friend, I'm sure it wasn't
that.

DERVISH. No, something even more absurd! For the
first time in my life it was flattery that trapped me.
It was the sincere and humane spirit of Saladin that
overpowered my resistance.

NATHAN. Flattery? What flattery?

DERVISH. "Only a beggar can read the soul of beg-
gars," stated Saladin, "only a beggar can know how
alms must rightly be distributed. Your predecessor,"
he said, "was far too cold, too gruff, and, if he gave
at all, a frown was on his brow. Every wretch was
thoroughly screened and questioned first in an imper-
ious manner. Not satisfied to know the poor man's need,
this officious man demanded first to know exactly how
his want arose. He then doled out a paltry pittance
in keeping with the cause. I know Al-Hafi won't do
that," he said, "nor will Saladin, I'm sure, appear
kind in such boorish ways, when you, Al-Hafi, take
over. Al-Hafi's not like a foul and clogged-up pipe,
yielding in mud and foam what it received as water,
pure and clean. No, definitely not! Al-Hafi thinks
and feels as I do." This was the pleasant tune the
fowler's luring pipe played in my ear, until the silly
bird was caught. O, what a fool I've been! Fool of a
fool, that's what I am!

NATHAN. Easy there, easy, please, my dervish.
You blame yourself too much.

DERVISH. Why tell me that? I ask you, Nathan,
isn't it rank foolery to crush men underfoot by the
tens of thousands, starve, rob, enslave, lash, stab,
and crucify them, then play the kindly benefactor to a
mere handful of these same oppressed wretches? Isn't
it rank foolery, yes, even blasphemy, to ape the mercy
of Almight God, who sends both sun and rain upon the
evil and the good alike, on wilderness and on culti-
vated lands? Isn't it absurd to ape Him and not have
the overflowing riches of Almighty God? Isn't it
utter folly?

NATHAN. Say no more, Al-Hafi, I understand your
feeling in this matter.

DERVISH. But, Nathan, my good friend, let me now know your views regarding my small part in this wild folly. Tell me, wouldn't I be just as great a fool in this utter foolery on Saladin's part to see only the good side? Should I play my part in this mad scheme of his merely for the sake of the good that's in it? Nathan, please answer me, I beg you.

NATHAN. What, Al-Hafi, you're asking me for counsel? Well then, so be it, here it is. My advice is that you return to the wilderness in all haste. With men you might forget the petty acts of so-called humane humans and learn again to be a man.

DERVISH. I fear that too. So long, friend Nathan!
                                                    (Exit)

NATHAN. What's this, Al-Hafi, on your way so fast? Surely you don't think the desert'll take wings and fly away. If only he'd wait a moment and listen to a friend! Al-l-l Ha-a-a-fi, please come back a moment! Oh, well, he's gone! I'd like very much to question him about our Templar, for very likely he knows all about him.

                        Scene iv

        [Enter DAJA in haste. NATHAN]

DAJA. Nathan! Nathan!

NATHAN. Yes, Daja? What's the matter now?

DAJA. We've seen him again! He's come back again!

NATHAN. Who, Daja? Who's come back again?

DAJA. *He*, Nathan, *he*!

NATHAN. All right, Daja, *he*! But who is *he*? Why
call him simply *he*? That's not proper, even if he is
an angel!

DAJA. He's pacing up and down beneath the palms
again and from the boughs he's picking dates as he
goes by.

NATHAN. You mean to say he's really *eating*?
You're quite sure he *is* a Templar?

DAJA. Please, Nathan, please don't tease me now!
If only you could have seen how eagerly she gazed
through the densely planted palms! She knew that he
was there, even before she saw him! If only you could
see how gratefully, how lovingly, her eyes now follow
him! She begs you to go to him at once and bring him
here to us. O, hurry, Nathan, please! From her window she'll soon make a sign to indicate which way he's
turning, whether he's near or farther away. Please
hurry, please!

NATHAN. How can I do that right away? My clothing's travel stained, the same as when I leaped down
from my camel. I'm not dressed to meet him, as you
see. Daja, hurry to him and tell him I've come home.
For, naturally, the worthy man's declined to come into
my home because the master of the house was absent.
Now he'll come right away, when I invite him. Go,
Daja, tell him I invite him with the greatest pleasure.

DAJA. That's all in vain! He'll not come, for —
in a word — he won't enter the house of any Jew!

NATHAN. Well then, if nothing else, just follow
him. Don't let him get away! Keep him in your sight!

I'll come at once!   (Nathan goes in and Daja leaves.)

                          Scene v

[The scene is an open space with palm trees, beneath
which the TEMPLAR is seen walking back and forth. A
FRIAR is following him at a distance on one side and
appears as if he wishes to address him.]

     TEMPLAR. He's following me again, as he did once
before. Look, now he's peering from behind his hands!
Good Brother, or perhaps I should say *Father*, tell me,
which is right?

     FRIAR. Just say *Brother*, nothing else, simply a
lay-brother at your service.

     TEMPLAR. Well now, Brother, if only I had any-
thing to give you! But, as God lives, I haven't ...

     FRIAR. No matter! My warmest thanks to you, good
friend, for your good will. May God give you a thou-
sandfold what you'd so gladly give. It's not the gift
that makes the giver, no, but rather his good will.
Besides, good friend, it's not to beg alms that I've
been sent to you.

     TEMPLAR. So you've been sent to me?

     FRIAR. Yes, I've been sent — from the cloister.

     TEMPLAR. Why, that's exactly where I'd hoped to
eat a simple pilgrim's meal!

     FRIAR. When I left, the table was already set.

So all you've got to do, good sir, is simply to come
back with me.

TEMPLAR.   Really, why should I? I haven't eaten
meat for many a day. What does it matter if I do or
if I don't? The dates, I find, are ripe.

FRIAR.   You must beware of this cold fruit. It's
quite unwholesome, greatly obstructing the spleen,
thickening the blood, and causing melancholy thoughts.

TEMPLAR.   That doesn't worry me. I'm prone to
melancholy and I welcome it. But surely you weren't
sent here to find me merely to warn me against eating
dates.

FRIAR.   No, I wasn't. I was sent here to learn
something about you, to sound you out and test you.

TEMPLAR.   And you're telling me this bluntly to
my face?

FRIAR.   Certainly, why shouldn't I?

TEMPLAR.   (Aside) A crafty Brother! Tell me, has
the cloister more like you?

FRIAR.   That I do not know, good sir, I must obey.

TEMPLAR.   And it's your custom there to listen and
obey and never question?

FRIAR.   I ask you, sir, how else could I *obey*?

TEMPLAR.   (Aside) How close simplicity often
comes to truth! (Aloud) You can confide in me. Now
tell me, first of all, who's the man who wants to know
me better? I'm sure it isn't you.

FRIAR. Would it become me, sir, or be to my advantage?

TEMPLAR. Well then, who's the man whom it becomes, this eager spying? To whose advantage is it to know me better?

FRIAR. In my opinion, it's the Patriarch. I'm sure he's the inquisitor, for he's the man who sent me here to pry on you.

TEMPLAR. Doesn't he know the red cross on a field of white?

FRIAR. Why, sir, even I know that!

TEMPLAR. Well, then, good friar, here's my story. I'm both a Templar and a prisoner. You'd like to know still more, I suppose? Well, I was captured at Tebnin, the fort which in the last hour of the truce we hoped to take and then press on to Sidon. Still more? Although twenty men were captured with me, Saladin spared my life alone. With this information, the Patriarch knows all he needs to know, yes, even more than necessary.

FRIAR. That's scarcely more than he knew yesterday. He'd also like to know the reason why you, only you, good knight, were pardoned by the Sultan.

TEMPLAR. How do I know why? Already I was kneeling, my mantle on the ground, and, with neck bared, was waiting for the death-stroke. Suddenly, with a searching look, Saladin sprang toward me. He gave a sign and I was raised up and unfettered. I turned to thank him, and then I saw his cheek was wet with tears. Amazed he stood there, and then he left me standing there equally dumbfounded. Your guess, good

Brother, is as good as mine what this strange riddle
means. The Patriarch too may guess, since he's so
interested.

FRIAR. He looks upon it in the light that God
most likely has great things in store for you.

TEMPLAR. O, yes, indeed, very great things! Such
things as rescuing a Jewish girl from a burning house
or guiding curious pilgrims to Mount Sinai! Truly
great things!

FRIAR. No doubt the "truly great things" will
also come in time. But, in the meantime, these present trifles have their value too. In fact, right now
the Patriarch himself has things of weightier import
to discuss with you, good knight.

TEMPLAR. Is this really so, my friend? Has he
mentioned anything to you? Are there any rumors you
have heard? Has he dropped a hint?

FRIAR. Oh, yes, quite definitely. But now, of
course, sir, you must first be tested to learn if
you're the right man for the job.

TEMPLAR. Tested, you say? You're going to test
me? (Aside) First of all we'll have to see just how
this testing goes! (Aloud) Well, sir, go on!

FRIAR. It seems to me the short way is the best,
so now I'll tell in plain words just what the Patriarch
has in mind for you.

TEMPLAR. Good Brother, I agree, please speak out
plainly.

FRIAR. He'd be very pleased if you, sir, would

be the man to bring a certain letter into the proper
hands.

TEMPLAR. I'm to deliver a letter? Tell me, my
friend, am I the Patriarch's errand-boy? Is this the
"truly great thing" planned for me, is this a worthier
business than snatching a young Jewess from the flames?

FRIAR. O, yes indeed, it is, and with good reason. You see, the Patriarch says this letter you're
to bear is so important that in it there's bound up
the whole of Christendom's fortune. "Carry this letter safely," the Patriarch says, "and you'll earn a
crown which by and by the King of Heaven'll give. That
crown," the Patriarch says, "no one is more worthy to
wear than you."

TEMPLAR. No one more worthy than I?

FRIAR. "No man on earth," the Patriarch says,
"can more surely wear that crown than you."

TEMPLAR. None more surely than I?

FRIAR. "He's got full freedom here, goes everywhere, is well aware how cities may be stormed and how
defended," the Patriarch says, "he can judge best the
weakness or the strength of Saladin's new inner fortress," the Patriarch says, "and in the plainest words
describe it to the army of the Christians."

TEMPLAR. Good friar, I'm wondering if I have the
right to hear both the content and the intent of the
Patriarch's letter.

FRIAR. The full content I don't know myself. I
do know that it's destined for King Philipp's hands.
The Patriarch — I must say I often wonder how a saint

who otherwise lives only in Heaven can stoop to be so
intimate with matters of this world. Such things
must sorely vex his soul!

TEMPLAR. I'm sure they must. But what were you
saying regarding the Patriarch?

FRIAR. He knows definitely and exactly how, where,
in what strength, and from what quarter Saladin will
re-open the campaign, in case the truce is broken and
the war renewed.

TEMPLAR. You say the Patriarch knows all this?

FRIAR. Yes, he does, and he'd be very glad if
King Philipp also knew it. If that were so, the King,
fortified with this knowledge, could judge whether the
risk was so great that the truce with Saladin — a
truce already broken by your Order — must be renewed
at any cost.

TEMPLAR. A fine Patriarch indeed! This fellow
wants no ordinary errand-boy in me. He'd like me as
a spy! Well, good Brother, tell your Patriarch this:
in testing me, you found me useless, wanting; I still
consider myself a prisoner and, most important of all,
the Templar's duty's always been to drive the foe before him with his naked spear, never to play the spy.

FRIAR. Just as I expected! And I don't blame
you, sir! But listen, please, the best is still to
come. The Patriarch has found out recently what the
stronghold's named and where it's built in Lebanon.
He also knows that in it there are hidden the untold
sums of money which Saladin's provident father stores
to pay the army and face the war's expense. To this
stronghold Saladin goes from time to time by devious
roads with only a small escort. Do you follow me? Do

you get the picture, my friend?

TEMPLAR. No, good friar, no, I don't.

FRIAR. Why, it's a simple matter then to ambush
Saladin, take him prisoner, and put him to death.
What could be easier? You're shuddering, sir? Well,
I can tell you this: two God-fearing Maronites have
offered voluntarily to carry out the deed, if only
some gallant man is to be found to guide them to the
Sultan.

TEMPLAR. And I'm the Patriarch's choice to do him
this great service!

FRIAR. Then he's sure that from Ptolemais King
Philipp will send assistance.

TEMPLAR. Friar, you're telling this to *me*?
Haven't you heard or is this the first time you hear
about the great debt of obligation by which I'm bound
to Saladin?

FRIAR. I've heard the story.

TEMPLAR. And still he's chosen me?

FRIAR. The Patriarch thinks that that's all well
and good, but God's rights and your Order ...

TEMPLAR. ... Change nothing! Surely, good friar,
you're not suggesting that I should be a scoundrel behind the Sultan's back!

FRIAR. No, no, by my faith! But, you see, the
Patriarch thinks a shabby trick in the sight of men
need not be one in the sight of God.

TEMPLAR. Which means that even though I owe my
life to Saladin, in God's sight it's quite all right
for me to kill him in return?

FRIAR. Oh, what's the use? The Patriarch looks
upon Saladin as a foe of Christendom and as such he
can have no claim to be your friend.

TEMPLAR. What do you mean, my *friend*? Need he be
my *friend* that I refuse to be his assassin, his thank-
less murderer?

FRIAR. Of course, good sir, I understand! But
the Patriarch thinks that we're not bound by thanks
either to God or man, when mercy shown was not for our
sake shown. Now rumor has it, you know, that the Sultan spared your life because he saw his brother's likeness in your face and manner.

TEMPLAR. So your fine Patriarch knows this too,
and still he'd have me play the murderer? If only it
were true! Oh, good Saladin, if Nature formed in me
one feature only like your brother's, shouldn't something in me likewise think of you the same way, namely as a brother? And this something in my soul, surely you don't think I'll change it merely to please
your Patriarch. No, no, my friend, Nature doesn't
lie. God doesn't contradict Himself in His own works!
Go, good friar, go! Don't make me angry! Let me
think this whole thing over!

FRIAR. I'm going, sir, going happier than I came.
I hope you'll pardon me, good friend. You understand,
I'm sure, we cloister brothers are under strictest
rule! We must obey those over us, our heads!

Scene vi

[The TEMPLAR and DAJA. DAJA has been watching the TEM-
PLAR for some time at a distance and now approaches
him.]

DAJA. (Aside) It looks to me as if the friar has
left him in a bad humor. But I must risk bringing him
my message just the same.

TEMPLAR. A fine state of affairs! Who'll say the
proverb lies that *a woman and a monk are the devil's
two claws*? Today he's tossing me from one to the
other.

DAJA. What's this I see? Is it really you, brave
knight? Thank God! I thank Him for His grace!
You've been in hiding so very long! You've not stayed
away because of illness, I hope.

TEMPLAR. No.

DAJA. You're in good health, then?

TEMPLAR. Yes.

DAJA. We've had much trouble, sir, because of
you.

TEMPLAR. Oh, really? Is that so?

DAJA. You were, I suppose, on a trip?

TEMPLAR. That's right, I was.

DAJA. And you've come back today?

TEMPLAR. No, yesterday.

DAJA. Today Recha's father came back too, so
surely Recha now dare hope ...

TEMPLAR. Hope for what?

DAJA. For what she's begged you now so often.
She's begging you to come to her. Her father himself
now invites you to his home most urgently. He's just
now returned from Babylon with richly-laden camels,
the costliest spices, precious jewels, and gorgeous
cloths that only India, Persia, Syria or China can
provide.

TEMPLAR. I'm very sorry, but I'm not interested
in buying.

DAJA. He's honored by his people as if he were a
prince. But still, I often wonder why the honored
title they give him is *Nathan the Wise*, not *Nathan the
Rich*.

TEMPLAR. You wonder why? Well, to his people
rich and *wise* are perhaps the same.

DAJA. It's my opinion that the name *Nathan the
Good* would've suited him much better. No words can
describe how good he really is. The moment when he'd
learned what Recha owed to you, there's nothing he
wouldn't have done for you or given you.

TEMPLAR. That's very likely true.

DAJA. Why not come with me and find out for yourself?

TEMPLAR. Why should I do that? I'm well aware

how quickly one forgets a moment such as that!

DAJA. Do you suppose, if it weren't so, if Nathan
weren't the good man I claim he is, that I'd have
stayed in his house for so long a time? Do you suppose that otherwise I'd forget my Christian worth? O,
no, it wasn't forecast at my cradle that I'd come to
Palestine with my lawful husband merely to be companion to a Jewish girl. My husband, you must know, was
a noble squire in Emperor Frederick Barbarossa's army.

TEMPLAR. I know, I know! He was a Swiss by birth
and had the honor conferred upon him to drown in the
selfsame river as His Imperial Majesty. Woman, do you
realize how often you've already told me this same
tale? Please, won't you finally stop running after
me?

DAJA. Running after you? O, good God!

TEMPLAR. Yes, I repeat, running after me. Once
and for all, I don't want to see you again or hear
from you any more. Nor do I constantly want to be
reminded of a deed in which my heart played no part
at all, a deed which even to myself becomes a riddle
when I think of it. Of course, I don't regret it ...
But, I'm telling you here and now, if the same decision were again before me, you'd be to blame if
I'd act less rashly, if I'd enquire first before I'd
act, and let burn what would.

DAJA. O, sir, you can't mean that! No God forbid!

TEMPLAR. From this day onward — I beg you —
do me this one favor: stay away from me. In my
book a Jew's a Jew. Keep the father away from me as
well, please, that's what I'm asking you. I'm a

rough and ready fellow, as you see. The girl's image is out of my mind long, long ago, if it was ever there.

DAJA. Well, I can tell you this: yours has never left her mind.

TEMPLAR. If that's the case, what can be done? Tell me, what do you think?

DAJA. Who knows? Men aren't always what they seem.

TEMPLAR. That's true, but they're seldom better. (He turns to go.)

DAJA. Please, wait a moment. Why this haste?

TEMPLAR. Woman, ever since I've come here I've loved these palms and their green shade. You've made them hateful.   (Exit)

DAJA. Go then, you German bear![2] Begone! I'll follow just the same in order not to lose you from my sight.   (Follows at a distance)

[END OF ACT ONE]

---

[2]The expression, *a German bear,* was the common designation of the serious, obstinate and gruff German prototype and became almost proverbial.

ACT TWO

Scene i

[The scene takes place in the Sultan's Palace.
SALADIN and SITTAH are playing chess.]

SITTAH. Look where you've moved to now, Saladin!
You're dreaming!

SALADIN. I thought I'd made a good move.

SITTAH. Yes, good for me! Well, do it over.

SALADIN. Why should I?

SITTAH. Your knight's left unprotected.

SALADIN. That's true. So what?

SITTAH. That forks your pawns and ...

SALADIN. In that case, I'll call check!

SITTAH. What good will that do? See, I'll simply cover it, and you'll be as badly off as you were
before.

SALADIN. I see no other way out of this predica-
ment except to make some sacrifice. Very well, then,
take my knight.

SITTAH. I don't want your knight. I'll pass.

SALADIN. Thanks for nothing! You've certainly

got a better strategy in mind to leave my knight in
place.

SITTAH. That could well be!

SALADIN. Don't make your reckoning without your
host. Just look here! Aren't you overlooking what
you'd gain?

SITTAH. Not at all. I can't imagine that you
think so little of your queen.

SALADIN. I think little of my queen?

SITTAH. I see very clearly that today I'll not
win my thousand dinars. Today I'll not win a penny.

SALADIN. And why do you think that?

SITTAH. Can you ask? Because, in spite of all
your cunning and all your skill, you're trying to lose.
But I won't let you! Such a deception isn't very
entertaining and, moreover, haven't I always won the
most money from you in games that I've lost? Then, to
comfort me for losing, you've always given me twice
our bet.

SALADIN. In that case, my dear, you should try
with all your might to lose.

SITTAH. Then probably it's your generosity, dear
brother, that's to blame, if I play badly, play to lose.

SALADIN. Let's stop our game! It's getting late,
we'll end it now!

SITTAH. And leave it as it is? Well, then,
check! and double check!

SALADIN. Well, now, I must say, I didn't see that move — That takes my queen as well —

SITTAH. Could you play otherwise? Let's see?

SALADIN. No, no, let's not do that! I must give up the queen! I've never been lucky with this piece!

SITTAH. Only with this piece?

SALADIN. Take it off! It's no good to me! Now all is covered as before.

SITTAH. You've often told me how courteously one must deal with queens ... (She lets the queen stand)

SALADIN. Take it or leave it, I've got no move.

SITTAH. Take it? Why should I? Check! Check!

SALADIN. Go on.

SITTAH. Well, then, check! and check! and check!

SALADIN. And mate!

SITTAH. Oh, no, you don't! You can move that man between, or make whatever move you like! It's all the same thing anyhow!

SALADIN. All right, you've won! I'll have Al-Hafi pay you right away! Let him be called! Sittah, you guessed the truth, my mind wasn't on the game. I was very absent-minded today! Besides, who always gives us these polished pieces, all smoothed away to nothing? A loser, you know, needs some excuse or other. No, no, Sittah, it wasn't the worn-down pieces made me lose, it was your skill, your swift and quiet moves ...

SITTAH. So that's the way you're trying to excuse
the embarrassment you feel because you've lost! Very
well, brother, you're distracted, even more than I am.
That I can believe.

SALADIN. Than you! What's distracting you?

SITTAH. Certainly not your distractions. O,
Saladin, when will we again be serious when we play
our game?

SALADIN. We'll play it all the more seriously
when the right time comes! Ah, now that the war's
been resumed, you mean? Well, let it start again!
Advance! Attack! I didn't want it, for — you see —
I hoped I could prolong the truce. My reasons? I
wanted very much to find a man for my dear Sittah!
In short, it's Richard's brother that I had in mind.
Think, dear sister, Richard's brother!

SITTAH. Will you never stop talking in praise of
Richard?

SALADIN. If our dear brother Melek, later on,
took Richard's sister for his wife, ah, what a glori-
ous royal house we'd make together! We'd be the first
and best of all the first and best outstanding royal
houses in the world! You note, I'm sure, that I'm not
lacking self-conceit as well, when I declare myself
quite worthy of my friends — Ah, what men such mat-
ings would produce!

SITTAH. Haven't I often laughed at this fine
dream of yours? You don't know Christians, and you'll
never know them. Their pride's not to be *men*, its to
be *Christians*. Even humanity — which from the days
of their dear Lord Jesus Christ has lessened superstition — they love, not for its human quality, but only
because Christ taught it and showed it in His deeds.

It is indeed a blessing that He was so good a man, a
man in whose virtues they can place their entire
faith! But are His virtues really theirs? No, not at
all, it's not His virtues but His name that they attempt to spread throughout the world and, in so doing,
cloud with slander and obliterate the names of all
good men. The name alone is everything to these
Christians.

SALADIN. By this you mean, no doubt, their condition that you and Melek both must first be Christian
converts, before a Christian marriage can be discussed.

SITTAH. Exactly! As if Christians alone were
capable of understanding the meaning of love, with
which Almighty God has endowed every man and woman on
this earth!

SALADIN. Christians believe so many ridiculous
things, that they can swallow even this absurdity!
But still, in this you are mistaken. The Templars are
the ones who are to blame, for they alone frustrate
our hopes. They won't yield up that pleasant town
which Richard's sister ought to bring to Melek as her
bridal dowry. They're hanging on to Acre for dear
life. In order not to lose the privilege of the
knight, they play the role of monk besides, the simple
monk! Believing they may shoot a lucky arrow at the
bird in flight, they scarcely can wait for the truce
to end! If that's the way they want to play, well
then, so be it! I'm ready for them! Advance, men,
and attack! If only other things were as they should
be!

SITTAH. Oh? Tell me, what else is troubling you?
What's not in order? What's on your mind that makes
you tremble so?

SALADIN. Why, precisely the same thing that's
made me tremble all along. I was in Lebanon lately,
as you know, and found our good father faltering
beneath his sore burdens.

SITTAH. O, that's a shame!

SALADIN. He can't go on. There's pressure everywhere. Whichever way we turn there's failure.

SITTAH. What failure? What brings about this
pressure that you speak of?

SALADIN. I'm almost ashamed to name it. When I
have it, this thing seems quite superfluous, and when
I need it, then it's indispensable. Where's Al-Hafi?
Has no one gone to get him? Pitiful, accursed money!
Ah, Al-Hafi, you're just the man I want to see!

Scene ii

[The dervish AL-HAFI. SALADIN. SITTAH.]

AL-HAFI. I think the money's now arrived, the
money from Egypt! May Allah grant that it be plenti-
ful!

SALADIN. Have you any news?

AL-HAFI. I? No, that I haven't. I thought I'd
get some here.

SALADIN. Pay Sittah the bet -- a thousand dinars.
                    (Paces up and down in thought.)

AL-HAFI. Pay? All I do is pay, pay, pay, but I
don't receive. A fine mess! Instead of something,
even less — even less than nothing. Pay Sittah, you
say, always Sittah! You've lost, I suppose? Lost
again and again at chess! Why, there's the board!

SITTAH. Surely you don't begrudge me my good
luck!

AL-HAFI. (Examining the board) Why begrudge you?
If — only you knew the truth!

SITTAH. (Signaling to him) Keep quiet, Al-Hafi,
quiet!

AL-HAFI. (Still examining the board) First of
all, don't begrudge your luck yourself.

SITTAH. Hush, Al-Hafi!

AL-HAFI. Were your pieces the white ones? Did
you call check on him?

SITTAH. It's a good thing he didn't hear you.

AL-HAFI. Was it his move next?

SITTAH. Say it out loud that you'll give me my
money.

AL-HAFI. Yes, yes, you'll get it, just as you always do.

SITTAH. What's that you're saying? Are you mad?

AL-HAFI. The game's not over yet. Saladin, you've
not lost it.

SALADIN. (Scarcely paying any attention) Pay
just the same, Al-Hafi, my good friend. We must pay.

AL-HAFI. Pay, pay, pay! Your queen's still
standing!

SALADIN. (Still preoccupied) That makes no difference, she's taken.

SITTAH. That's enough, Al-Hafi! Say that I can
have my money when I please.

AL-HAFI. (Still concentrating on the board) Just
as it always is! But even if your queen's been taken,
Saladin, you're still not checkmated because of that ...

SALADIN. (Steps up to the board and sweeps the
pieces to the floor.) I *am* check-mated. That's the
way I want it.

AL-HAFI. You're right! The object is to win, and
paying off the winner follows!

SALADIN. (To Sittah) What's he saying?

SITTAH. (Signaling to Al-Hafi when she can without Saladin seeing it) You know him, Saladin, how he
loves to argue and be asked — and — if I'm not mistaken, he's jealous too.

SALADIN. Surely not of you — surely not of you,
dear sister. What's this I hear, my Hafi, jealous?

AL-HAFI. Could be, could be, you know! I'd gladly have a brain like hers myself and such a heart.

SITTAH. But none-the-less he pays off honestly.
He'll do the same today, you can depend on that! Now

go, Al-Hafi, go! Shortly I'll send someone to you to get the money.

AL-HAFI. No, I'll no longer play a part in this mad pantomime, this farce. Sooner or later he'll have to learn the truth.

SALADIN. Learn the truth? Who? What truth?

SITTAH. Is this the way you keep your promise, Al-Hafi? Don't break your oath to me!

AL-HAFI. Could I imagine it would go as far as this?

SALADIN. Come, come, what's up? Speak out! Tell me too!

SITTAH. I beg you, Al-Hafi, be discreet!

SALADIN. Well, I must say, this is indeed a strange affair! Sittah confides a solemn, earnest matter to a stranger, to a dervish, and not to me, her brother. Solve this riddle now, at once, Al-Hafi, I command you! Tell me all, dervish!

SITTAH. Please don't let a trifle work you up, dear brother, more than it warrants. Lately, as you know, once or twice I've won a bet from you like this at chess. Well, I've no urgent need just now for that money and, besides, Al-Hafi's treasury's not exactly full. Messengers with money haven't come yet either, as I know. But don't you worry, Saladin, for I'm not making this a gift to you, dear brother, or to Al-Hafi, or his treasury!

AL-HAFI. If only that were all!

SITTAH. And other trifles such as that! But I haven't touched the money that you once set apart for me. For quite a few months now it's remained untouched.

AL-HAFI. But that's not all!

SALADIN. Not *all*? Well, then, tell me *all*!

AL-HAFI. Ever since the time that we've been waiting for the gold from Egypt, she's ...

SITTAH. Don't listen to him, brother!

AL-HAFI. ... she's not only not taken anything for herself ...

SALADIN. What an excellent, devoted sister! She's even helped out with her own. Am I right?

AL-HAFI. Quite right! In fact, she's maintained your entire court, and borne the whole expenditure alone!

SALADIN. Just as I thought! That's my sister! (Kisses her)

SITTAH. Well, now, who made me rich enough to do such things but you, dear brother?

AL-HAFI. Who'll also make you poor as any beggar, as he now is himself.

SALADIN. I'm *poor*? Her brother *poor*? When have I ever had more than I have now? When have I had less? One coat, one sword, one steed and, finally, — one God. What more, I ask you, should I need or want? When shall I not have these? And yet, Al-Hafi, I've good reason to find fault with you.

SITTAH. Don't blame him, Saladin. If only I
could likewise lessen our dear father's burden as much
as yours!

SALADIN. Ah, now you dash my joy right to the
ground again! Although there's nothing I myself am
lacking or can lack, it's his need that's the greatest, and it's with him that we must suffer now. Oh,
what am I to do, now that our gold supplies from Egypt
are so late in coming? It may be a long time still
that we must wait for them and why, God only knows,
for there's no news from there. Cut down, draw in,
and save, all that I'll gladly do. Nothing will
please me better if in this it's I alone who suffer,
and no one else. For, in the end, what's really to be
gained by these supplies? I still must have my steed,
my coat, my sword. And with my God it's no hard task
for me to be on the very best of terms, for He's content with one small gift, namely my soul. — But I
must say, good Hafi, I counted a great deal on a surplus in your treasury.

AL-HAFI. A *surplus*? I'm sure that you'll confess
I'd been strangled, perhaps even impaled, if in vain
you had demanded this surplus of a bankrupt. Fraud
and embezzlement would then have been my last recourse.

SALADIN. Now, what can we do? Tell me, Hafi, why
did you turn to Sittah to borrow her small fortune?
Aren't there any others?

SITTAH. Could I let this privilege pass me by to
help you out, dear brother? Oh, no, I won't give up
this pleasure till I must. My fortune's not yet
wholly drained, you know.

SALADIN. But pretty nearly! This is the last
straw! It's all I needed to goad me on! At once,
good Hafi, make your plans! Get money now from anyone
you can! Don't quibble with me now on trivial details
regarding ways and means! Go forth directly now to
borrow and to pledge! But, good Hafi, don't borrow
from those people I made rich, for they might look
upon me as an Indian giver asking them to give back
that which I gave them. Ask those who're known as
covetous men, for they'll be willing right away, knowing, as they do, how fast with me their money multi-
plies.

AL-HAFI. I don't know anyone like that.

SITTAH. Didn't I hear right, Al-Hafi, that your
friend's returned home from his long trip?

AL-HAFI. A friend? A friend of mine? Who do you
mean by that?

SITTAH. The friend you praised so highly, your
friend the Jew.

AL-HAFI. I praised a Jew! You say a Jew was
praised by me?

SITTAH. "A man endowed by God with all the good
things of this world, the least and also the greatest
in abundance," — these were the words you once used
to describe him.

AL-HAFI. Did I say that? I wonder what I meant
by that?

SITTAH. The least was *wealth,* the greatest *wisdom.*

AL-HAFI. What are you saying? A Jew? I said
that of a Jew?

SITTAH. You couldn't say enough in praise of your good Nathan!

AL-HAFI. Oh, you're talking about *him*! You mean Nathan! Is that so, has he come home again at last? If you're right, then I'm sure his journey's been a prosperous one. And it's quite true that people speak of him as *the Wise* and know him as *the Rich*.

SITTAH. I'm quite aware of that, and now more than ever he's called *the Rich*. All Jerusalem's buzzing about the rarities, the gorgeous cloths and the precious jewels in his caravan.

AL-HAFI. Well, then *Nathan the Rich* has come back home, and with him comes, who knows, perhaps *the Wise* as well.

SITTAH. What's your opinion, Hafi? Couldn't you approach him?

AL-HAFI. Approach him for what purpose? Surely not to borrow? Ah, there you touch his sore spot! Nathan lend? Now that's precisely where his wisdom lies, for he'll not lend to any man.

SITTAH. That's not the picture you once drew of him.

AL-HAFI. To those in dire need, he'll lend his goods — but money? — money never! But otherwise, he's one Jew in a million. Nathan has brains, knows how to live, and plays good chess.[1] He's quite distinct in bad points and in good from other Jews. I'm

---

[1]Moses Mendelssohn, Lessing's good friend, is here referred to.

warning you, don't count on him. It's to the poor he
gives and just as freely — if not as largely — and
with as good a will as Saladin himself. This he does
without respect of persons — Christian and Jew,
Mussulman and Parsee, they're all alike to him.[2]

SITTAH. And such a man ...

SALADIN. Tell me, how is it I don't know this man
and haven't heard his name?

SITTAH. Wouldn't he lend to Saladin, a man whose
only care is for the wants of others, not his own?

AL-HAFI. That's where the Jew comes into play,
the common, vulgar Jew! And yet, you see, he envies
you the most precisely on the score of giving, so
jealous he's become. For himself he grabs all that
God offers of riches in this world. And for one reason only he'll not lend to anyone, namely, so he'll
have more to give. His reasoning goes like this:
The law commands him to give Charity, the law, however, doesn't command him to oblige a neighbor. So
Charity's the cause for making him the least oblig-
ing friend in the whole world. To tell the truth,
lately I've been on the outs with him, but all the
same don't think because of this that I'll speak ill
of him. He's good and kind — good in every way —
except for this one quirk. No, I'll not go to him
for this. I'll go at once and knock at other doors ...
and I've just this instant remembered a rich Moor, a
covetous man, and it's to him I'll go!

SITTAH. Hafi, Al-Hafi, why do you hurry so?

_____
[2]This is the very essence of tolerance, both religious and racial.

SALADIN. O, let him! Let him go!

Scene iii

[SITTAH. SALADIN.]

SITTAH. How hastily he leaves, as though he's glad to get away from me! What does it mean? I wonder? Has he really been deceived in Nathan, or are we — by any chance — the ones he's trying to deceive?

SALADIN. What do you mean *deceive*? You're asking me who hardly even know what your talk was all about. I've never heard until today about this Jew of yours, this Nathan.

SITTAH. How can a man possibly be unknown to you who, people say, has found the graves of David and of Solomon and with a secret password breaks their seals? From time to time, it's said, he brings forth inexhaustible treasures from these graves, which no lesser source could furnish.

SALADIN. If this man finds his wealth in graves, you may be sure they're not the graves of David or of Solomon. Fools are buried there!

SITTAH. Criminals, perhaps! Besides, the source of Nathan's wealth is far more fertile and inexhaustible than any grave of Mammon.

SALADIN. He's a merchant, isn't he? I believe that's what you told me.

SITTAH. On every highway his mule-trains may be

found, every desert has seen his caravans, his ships
are moored in every port. Al-Hafi once told me all
these things and in his joyful pride he added how
charitably and how nobly Nathan put to use the wealth
which he — wise as he is — did not disdain to earn
by his great industry and diligence. Continuing, he
boasted how free from prejudice is Nathan's soul, how
open is his heart to every virtue, how perfectly in
tune with all things beautiful! I tell you, Saladin,
Al-Hafi praised him to the skies!

SALADIN. Yet, when he spoke of him just now, he
seemed uncertain and cold toward this same Nathan ...

SITTAH. No, no, brother, not cold, but — if I
judge him right — I'd say perplexed, as though he
thought it dangerous to praise him, and could not
blame him undeservedly. Then too, could it not be
that the noblest Jew — unable to deny his race — is
still a Jew, and that this fact makes Al-Hafi ashamed
of his dear friend? Well, whatever his reason may be,
whether this Jew be more Jew or less Jew, what's that
to us — if only he's *rich*? As far as we're concerned, that's all that matters.

SALADIN. But, dear sister, surely you wouldn't
take from him by force that which belongs to him?

SITTAH. What do you mean *by force*? With fire and
sword? No, no, of course not, for with the weak the
only violence needed is their own weakness. But now
come to my harem for a while and hear the slave-girl
singer I bought yesterday. In the meantime, perhaps a
shrewd plan that I have in mind regarding this man
Nathan will mature. — Come!

Scene iv

[In front of Nathan's house where it's close to the
palm trees. Enter RECHA and NATHAN. DAJA comes to
join them.]

RECHA. O, father, you've been away so long! We
can scarcely hope to meet him now ...

NATHAN. Have no fear, my child, if not among the
palms, why then we'll find him somewhere else. Just
keep calm, don't get excited. But isn't that Daja
coming this way?

RECHA. O, she's lost him too! That's easy to
see.

NATHAN. How can you know that?

RECHA. Otherwise she'd hurry more in coming. She'd
be running.

NATHAN. Perhaps she hasn't seen us yet.

RECHA. Look, she sees us only now.

NATHAN. And now she's quickening her steps. Just
be calm, be calm!

RECHA. O, Nathan, would you expect a daughter to
be calm in such a case as this? Would you want me to
show no interest in the welfare of this man whose
brave deed saved my life, a life that's dear to me only
because I owe it all to you?

NATHAN. I'd want you to remain just as you are,
even if I were aware that something new and strange
was stirring in your loving breast.

RECHA. What can you mean, dear father?

NATHAN. You ask me that? Are you so shy, so
timid, with *me*? What's stirring now deep in your soul
is innocence and nature. Don't let it upset you, just
as I'm not at all upset by it. But when your heart
has spoken in a clearer voice, promise me, Recha,
you'll not keep your wishes from me.

RECHA. Of course, I won't! The very thought of
that almost makes me tremble, the thought that I might
wish to hide my thoughts from you.

NATHAN. Let's talk no more of this, it's over
once for all. Ah, here's Daja now. Well, Daja?

DAJA. He's still walking beneath the palms and
soon he'll come this way by that hedge over yonder.
Look, there he comes already!

RECHA. He appears uncertain which path to take,
right or left, uphill or down.

DAJA. No, he'll not go that way yet. First he'll
follow the footpath round the cloister once or twice
again and then he'll have to pass by here. What does
it matter anyhow?

RECHA. Tell me, Daja, did you speak to him already? How is he today?

DAJA. The same as always.

NATHAN. Watch out! Be careful! Don't be seen!

Go back a step or two or, better still, go in the
house.

RECHA. Let me have just one more look! Oh, what
a shame! The hedge hides him from me.

DAJA. Come, Recha, your father's right! Out here
you run the risk that he'll turn back at once, if he
should see you.

RECHA. Alas, alas, that the hedge should hide him
from my view!

NATHAN. If he should suddenly turn his eyes this
way, he's bound to see you. So, go in, please. Go in!

DAJA. Come, Recha, I know a window where it's
safe for us to see him.

RECHA. You do? Very well, Daja, let's go in!
                    (The two go into the house.)

                    Scene v

          [NATHAN and, presently, the TEMPLAR]

NATHAN. I almost shrink from this strange man.
His rugged virtues almost overwhelm me. How is it
that one man can so perplex another? He's coming. By
Heaven, this lad is a real man! I'm quite impressed
with his strong, defiant glance and his brave car-
riage! In this man, I'm sure, only the shell is bitter,
the kernel must be sweet. Where have I seen before a
man like him? Excuse me, noble Frank ...

TEMPLAR. What's that you're saying?

NATHAN. Excuse me ...

TEMPLAR. What do you want with me, Jew? Why
should I excuse you?

NATHAN. That I dare to greet you in this manner.

TEMPLAR. Tell me, can I prevent it? Well, make
it short.

NATHAN. Please, forgive my forwardness. Don't
pass by so hastily and scornfully and don't slight, I
beg you, a man who's bound to you eternally.

TEMPLAR. In what way are you bound to me? Oh,
I can almost guess! You're ...

NATHAN. My name is Nathan and I'm the young
girl's father, the girl your bravery rescued from the
fire. I've come to ...

TEMPLAR. If you've come to thank me — save your
breath! I've already had to suffer too much thanks
because of this mere trifle. You owe me nothing, I
assure you. How could I know the girl I rescued was
your daughter? It's our rule, you know, a Templar's
duty, to hasten to the aid of anyone who's in distress.
Besides, at the time my life to me seemed not worth
living. So, I gladly rushed in, snatching the opportunity to risk my own life to save another's life,
even if it turned out to be only the life of a Jewish
girl.

NATHAN. Yes indeed, that's the true hero's way!
He does great deeds but doesn't boast about them!
He'd rather hide behind his modesty merely to avoid

applause! But when he scoffs at the praise I give in
heartfelt gratitude, tell me, what offering won't he
scorn? And, good Templar, if you weren't a stranger
and a prisoner here, I certainly wouldn't talk to you
so boldly. Command me, I beg you, how can I serve
you?

TEMPLAR. Serve *me*? In no way at all.

NATHAN. As you can see, I'm rich.

TEMPLAR. But in my eyes a rich Jew was never a
better Jew.

NATHAN. Because of that would you ignore a man,
reject the good he has within him, and take no help
from his full hands?

TEMPLAR. No, as for that, I'll swear no oaths,
even on my Templar's mantle. When in time it won't be
only partly worn as now, but merely rags and threadbare,
when seams and stitches will no longer hold, why then
perhaps I'll come to you to borrow money or else cloth
to change it for a new one. — Don't look at it so
closely! Don't worry, you're still safe, it's not yet
that far gone! It's still in fairly good condition!
There's just one bad spot on the lappet here where it
was singed. That burned spot came about when from the
searing flames I carried out your daughter.

NATHAN. (Takes hold of the lappet and gazes at
it.) It is a wondrous thing for sure, that this foul
spot, this spot singed by the fire, should show this
man's true worth much better than his own words do. I
must kiss it now, this foul spot singed by fire! Forgive me, sir, I didn't mean to do it.

TEMPLAR. Forgive? What?

NATHAN. A tear fell on the spot.

TEMPLAR. Think nothing of it. It's had more
drops than that. — (Aside) This Jew, I fear, will
soon bewilder me.

NATHAN. Could I be so bold, I wonder, to ask you
for a favor? Would you mind to send this mantle to my
child?

TEMPLAR. My mantle? Why?

NATHAN. So she can also press her lips upon this
spot. Though she hopes in vain, it is her fervent
wish to thank you too — in person. She would embrace
your knees!

TEMPLAR. But you're a Jew! Your name, you say,
is Nathan? — Why, Nathan, you've spoken such kind
words, such delicate words, to me, you've really
startled me ... Why certainly ... I'd ...

NATHAN. Sham and pose as you like, my friend!
I've found you out! You're too good, too modest, to
be more courteous. Your feelings for the girl in her
sad plight were — personally — all zeal to serve.
But since her father was so far away, your only care
was the preservation of her good name. You therefore
fled temptation, fled it so that you would not win her
in this way. And now, good sir, I'm thinking you ...

TEMPLAR. You know, I see, how we Knight Templars
think.

NATHAN. Only Templars? Only they? And only because your Order has a rule commanding this? No,
Templar, I know how *good* men think and I also know

that there are *good* men in all countries.[3]

TEMPLAR. Well, yes, of course, but there are differences none-the-less!

NATHAN. That's true, differences in color, dress,
and form.

TEMPLAR. These differences, you'll admit, are
greater or lesser in the various different climates on
our earth.

NATHAN. Distinctions such as these to me are very
small. In every land great men need great spheres and,
when such plants become too densely planted, they
branch off elsewhere in search of better sites. But
on the other hand, the average men like us are massed
together in all lands. In their case, one must not
suppress, must not humiliate the others! The halt
must tolerate the lame, the hill must not be arrogant
and vaunt itself the only lofty mountain in the world![4]

TEMPLAR. That's most nobly said! But, Nathan,
are you not aware which people first scoffed at all
others? Don't you know which nation first proclaimed
itself *the chosen race*? Tell me, what if I couldn't
help it — not hating, exactly — but holding these
people in low esteem due to their overweening pride?

---

[3] This is indeed a significant statement, one which people everywhere
should bear in mind and take to heart.

[4] This is the acme of racial tolerance. It shows clearly how far-
sighted and ahead of his time Lessing really was. In our twentieth
century of racial strife, Lessing's words seem like a cool, fresh
breeze of understanding.

Their pride, which they passed on to Moslems and to
Christians too that their God and theirs alone is the
one true God. It startles you, I see, to hear a
Christian and a Templar talk this way. But tell me,
when and where has this pious madness to impose this
better God on the whole world ever before been shown
in a blacker form than right here and now? The scales
must fall from the dimmed eyes of anyone who thinks
about this matter. Well, let those be blind, who
will! Forget what I've just said and I'll be off.

                                        (Starts going.)

   NATHAN. Come, good Templar, don't you know how
much more firmly my hold is on you now, how very much
I really want your friendship? Despise my people if
you like, but this you surely know: neither you nor
I have chosen our people. Well, then, are *you*, am *I*,
our people? People? What do we really mean when we
say the *people*? Are Jew and Christian first Jew and
Christian before they're *men*?[5] Alas, if only I'd
found in you one more who'd be content simply to be
called a *men*!

   TEMPLAR. By Heaven, Nathan, you've found a *man*,
you have! Give me your hand in friendship. I'm deeply ashamed to have mistaken you even for one moment!

   NATHAN. I'm proud of it, for only common things
are seldom misjudged.

   TEMPLAR. And things that are so rare one seldom
can forget. Yes, yes, Nathan, by all means, we must
indeed be friends.

---

[5]This is an eloquent plea for tolerance, racial and religious.
Lessing states correctly that the individual's worth is all-
important, not his ancestry or his religion, as far as tolerance is
concerned.

NATHAN. That, good Templar, we are already. Oh,
how glad will Recha be! What a joyous future now
opens up in my mind's eye! Just wait until you know
her! You'll see how good, how kind, she really is!

TEMPLAR. My heart's on fire in my breast. Who's
running from your doorway over there? Isn't it your
Daja?

NATHAN. It is. She's agitated and seems troubled!

TEMPLAR. Can it be that Recha's had an accident?

Scene vi

[The former, and DAJA, in great haste]

DAJA. O, Nathan! Nathan!

NATHAN. Well, what is it?

DAJA. Pardon me, good Templar, for breaking in
this way upon your conversation.

NATHAN. Well, well? What's the matter now?

DAJA. A message from the Sultan has arrived. He
wants to speak with you. My God, Nathan, the Sultan!

NATHAN. With me? The Sultan? Likely he's curious
to see the novelties I've brought back from abroad.
Tell him simply there's only very little or else that
almost nothing's been unpacked as yet.

DAJA. No, no, Nathan, no! He doesn't want to see

these things. He wants to talk to you, to you in
person, now without delay.

NATHAN. I'll come at once. You return to Recha.

DAJA. Don't take offense at us, good Templar, for
we're deeply troubled, not knowing what the Sultan's
up to.

NATHAN. Well, we'll soon find out. Go, Daja,
please go in!   (Daja leaves.)

Scene vii

[NATHAN and the TEMPLAR]

TEMPLAR. I take it you don't know him yet, personally I mean.

NATHAN. The Sultan? No, not yet. Though I've
never avoided him, I've never gone out of my way to
meet him either. The general public's spoken so highly in his praise, that my opinion must be based on
rumor rather than on personal observation. But now,
even if the opposite were true, by sparing your life
he's ...

TEMPLAR. Very true! There you speak the truth!
The life I now enjoy was given to me by him —

NATHAN. And, by doing so, he's given me a double,
threefold life. I confess here and now that this has
altered all between us. It's thrown a cord around me,
so to speak, which binds me both to him and to his
service. Now I can hardly wait to know what he com-

mands. I'm ready now for anything, and also ready to
tell him what I do for him I really do for your sake.

TEMPLAR. I haven't had a chance to thank him
either, though I've often tried to do so, but in vain.
The impression I made on him, you see, came like a
flash of lightning and vanished just as fast. Who
can even tell whether he still remembers me? And yet
he must once more at least call me before him to fix
my fate. For me it's not enough that I'm still alive
at his command and by his will. I must find out from
him what plan he's got in mind for me and in what role
I am to spend my days.

NATHAN. That you must, so I'll delay no longer.
Perhaps there'll be an opening in our talk for me to
speak of you. So, if you'll now allow me to excuse
myself, I'll be off to Saladin. When can we count
on seeing you at my home?

TEMPLAR. When may I come?

NATHAN. Whenever you please.

TEMPLAR. Why, then I'll come today.

NATHAN. And, may I ask, what is your name?

TEMPLAR. My name was formerly — before I joined
the Templars — Curt von Stauffen — Curt!

NATHAN. Von Stauffen? Stauffen? Stauffen!

TEMPLAR. You're startled? Why are you so surprised?

NATHAN. Stauffen! There are, I know, many
families which have that name.

TEMPLAR. Here in this very earth several men who
bore that name are resting now and rotting. My uncle
— no, my father, as I call him — is one... Why do
you look at me so strangely, Nathan, so searchingly?

NATHAN. It's nothing, nothing at all! How can I
ever tire of looking at you, my friend? And now I
leave you for this cause.

TEMPLAR. A searcher's eye, you know, not seldom
finds more than it seeks. Nathan, frankly this makes
me wonder. Let our friendship develop gradually, if
you will, not watching every glance. (He leaves.)

NATHAN. What did he say? "Searchers often find
more than they seek." It was as if he'd read my mind!
It's really true, this too might come to pass! He's
got not only Wolf's build and Wolf's walk, but Wolf's
voice too. The way he moves his head — Wolf to the
life! The bearing of his sword upon his arm, the
stroking of his eyebrows, just as Wolf did, to hide
the intensity of his fiery gaze! How clearly such
images still lie dormant till some word or other, some
tone, recalls them to the mind. Von Stauffen! right,
right, Filnek and Stauffen — I'll get to the bottom
of this matter very soon, but now I must be off to
meet with Saladin. But first let's check! I'll bet
our Daja's been in hiding and listening all this time.
Come out, Daja, come out!

Scene viii

[DAJA, NATHAN]

NATHAN. What are you up to now? Today there's
something prompting both your hearts for news that's
altogether different than my interview with Saladin.

DAJA. Well, Nathan, can you blame her? You and
the Templar were beginning to talk much friendlier
just when the Sultan's message came, causing us to
leave our window hideaway.

NATHAN. You can tell her now that she can look
for him to come at any moment. He's promised me he
would.

DAJA. For sure? O, Nathan, are you sure?

NATHAN. Daja, I've always trusted you and I'll go
on trusting you. Be on your guard, be dutiful and
true and, above all, have no regrets of conscience
after it's too late. Be very sure that you don't ruin
one single point in all my plans. Continue still to
discuss and question as you always have with lady-like
modesty and proper reserve ...

DAJA. O, Nathan, to think that you can still
remember our differences of opinion at such a time!
I'll go, and you must also go, for, as you see,
Saladin's second messenger, Al-Hafi, your good dervish, is coming in great haste.

Scene ix

[NATHAN, AL-HAFI]

AL-HAFI. Well, well! You're just the man I'm
looking for.

NATHAN. What's your big hurry? What does he want
with me?

AL-HAFI. Who?

NATHAN. Saladin, of course. Tell him I'm coming.
I'm on my way.

AL-HAFI. Who? Saladin?

NATHAN. Naturally. Didn't he send you here?

AL-HAFI. Me? No. Has he sent for you already?

NATHAN. Yes, that he has.

AL-HAFI. Then everything's all right.

NATHAN. What do you mean by that? What's all
right?

AL-HAFI. I'll not be blamed for this. God knows,
I'm not to blame. What all haven't I said and lied
about you to get him off your scent, to get you off
the hook!

NATHAN. To get me off what hook?   What do you
mean *all right*?

AL-HAFI.· Nathan, what I'm telling you is simply
this: you're Saladin's right-hand man now, you're his
treasurer! I must say I pity you! I won't stay to
see you be the toy of Saladin. This very hour I'm
leaving Saladin's service. You know already where I'm
going and you know the way. Perhaps there's something
I can do for you to help you out now that I'm on my
way. I'm at your service, as you know. It must, of
course, be limited to what one naked man can carry on
his back. You need only speak. I'm leaving right
away.

NATHAN. Just a moment, Al-Hafi, stop a moment,
please. As yet I know nothing at all about these

matters which worry you so much. First tell me,
please, what does all this mean?

AL-HAFI. You'll bring the sack along, of course.

NATHAN. The sack?

AL-HAFI. Why, the gold you'll lend to Saladin.

NATHAN. Oh, is that all?

AL-HAFI. Perhaps you'd like me to look on and
watch him bleed you white? See the waste of his fine
charity draw from the barns once full and draw again
and again, until the wretched natives and even the
very mice are starved? Do you dream perhaps that
Saladin, who's thirsting now to take your gold from
you, will also follow your advice? Ha! that man follow counsel! Since when has Saladin let himself be
counselled? When has he ever taken anyone's advice?
Just imagine, Nathan, what I chanced to see just now!

NATHAN. What was that, Al-Hafi?

AL-HAFI. I happened to come in as he was playing
chess with his sister Sittah. She's a skillful player,
but the game, which Saladin had given up as lost, still
stood upon the board. As I glanced over the board, I
saw that this game was as yet neither lost nor won.

NATHAN. That was a rare discovery for you. I'll
bet you were excited!

AL-HAFI. All Saladin had to do was move his king
on pawn to give his sister check. If I could only
show you!

NATHAN. I'll take your word for it.

AL-HAFI. The rook would then be freed and she'd
be done. I wished to show him this and called him to
the board. Imagine what he did!

NATHAN. He didn't agree with you, I'll bet!

AL-HAFI. He wouldn't even listen, and in his
anger and contempt he swept the chess-pieces to the
floor!

NATHAN. Is that really so?

AL-HAFI. Yes, that's so. In a sudden rage he
said that this time at least for once he'd take check-
mate, for that's the way he wished it. Tell me,
Nathan, can that be called good play?

NATHAN. Hardly, I'm sure! That's playing with
the play.

AL-HAFI. In my opinion, such play's not worth a
rotten filbert.

NATHAN. Money, more or less, that matters little
or nothing. But not to listen to you, not even to
listen, concerning so important a point, not to admire
and praise your eagle-eye, that — I would say — demands revenge. Don't you agree?

AL-HAFI. You're joking with me now! I've told you
this to give you some idea how his mind often works.
In short, I'm sick and tired of his whims and wash my
hands as far as he's concerned. I'm done with him!
In his service here, I'm running among filthy Moors
begging for the loan of filthy money. I, who never in
my life begged for myself, I'm now begging and borrowing for him. Borrowing's pretty nearly as bad as begging and lending money at such usury just about as bad

as stealing. Among my people on the banks of the
Ganges, I'll have no need to either beg or borrow,
nor need I be the instrument of one or of the other.
Only by the Ganges you'll find *men,* but here — except yourself — there's no man worthy of the honor
to live upon its banks. So come with me, friend
Nathan, and leave to Saladin his plunder to dispose
as he sees fit and at his will. I'm warning you,
he'll bring you step by step to abject beggary and
squander all your worldly goods. I'll gladly be
your guide and guarantor. I beg you, Nathan, come!

NATHAN. I'm inclined to agree with you, my friend,
it might be our last resort. But, Hafi, I must think
it over. Please, wait until ...

AL-HAFI. Think it over? Such matters can't be
put off and thought over.

NATHAN. ... until I come back from Saladin, until
I've taken leave ...

AL-HAFI. To hesitate and ponder is merely an excuse for one who fears to dare. The man who cannot
instantly decide to live a life of freedom must live a
slave to other men forever. Do as you please! Decide
as you think best! My way lies over yonder, yours
here!

NATHAN. But, Hafi, surely you'll first settle
your treasurership with the Sultan!

AL-HAFI. You must be joking! The total of my
treasury's not even worth counting. And, I know,
Nathan, either you or else Sittah will be guaranty for
my account. So, farewell, my friend! (He leaves.)

NATHAN. Be guarantor for Al-Hafi! Yes, yes, I

know him well — savage, kind, and faithful! When all
is said and done, only the true beggar is really a
true king!

END OF ACT TWO

ACT THREE

Scene i

[In Nathan's house. RECHA and DAJA]

RECHA. Daja, what did my father say today? "You
can expect him any moment now?" Doesn't that sound
as if he'd come at once? Well, haven't a thousand
moments passed since then? But who remembers moments
that are past? My mind's made up to live for each
next moment now, for one will surely come when he'll
be here.

DAJA. O, that confounded message from the Sultan! Except for that, Nathan would have brought him
right away.

RECHA. When that moment that I've yearned for so
arrives at last, fulfilling all my tender wishes, what
then, Daja? What then?

DAJA. You're asking me, what then? Why, then
I'm hoping that my most tender wish will also be fulfilled.

RECHA. Tell me, Daja, what will take its place?
How will my heart learn to pound again without some
overpowering wish like this? And if there is none, to
me that's little short of terror!

DAJA. My wish will take its place if yours is not
fulfilled. I'd like to see you in safe hands in
Europe, hands that are worthy to look after you.

RECHA. That's wishful thinking, Daja! The very
reason why this wish is yours makes it impossible
ever to be mine. For you, of course, your country's
the magnet that attracts you. I ask you, shouldn't
mine keep me right here? Why should the thought of
seeing your loved ones give you joy, while I leave
mine behind and go with you?

DAJA. I know you'll fight against it, but, struggle as you will, the ways of Heaven are still as wonderful as they always were! Suppose, my dear, it
should turn out the God of that very Templar who saved
you from the flames would also lead you back to that
same soil where you were born?

RECHA. Daja, what strange talk is this? Your
brain's now hatching up the wildest fancies. *His* God,
you say? The *Templar's* God, the God that *he* defends?
Does God belong to *him* alone? What kind of God is
that belonging to one man, one who must be defended by
His faithful? No, Daja, no! Who can say for what
soil we were born, if we're not true to that land
where we were really born? I tell you, Daja, you
would really be in trouble if my father heard you talk
like this! I'd hate to hear what he'd say to you, who
always picture me and my happiness far away from him!
How he'd loathe you for the weeds and tares of your
own land, for mixing these so wantonly with the pure
seed of reason he's been sowing so faithfully in my
soul! No, dear Daja, no, he'll not allow your rank
weeds to take root upon my soil! But I must tell you
too, so beautiful are your blossoms, that I've felt
the fertile soil of my strong faith weakened and con-
sumed by them! In their overpowering fragrance, I've
felt my heart and brain grow dizzy and bewildered!
You — being used to them — can bear this fragrance!
Nor do I envy you your stronger nerves, nerves that
can stand it! But me it doesn't suit. Why, even your

guardian angel didn't really fool me! Here in my
father's house I'm actually ashamed to be a part of
such a folly!

    DAJA. Folly, you call it! As if all reason were
at home only here! Folly, you say, folly! You think
it's folly, do you? O, if I could only speak! If
only you knew the truth, my dear!

    RECHA. Well, why can't you speak? Tell me, Daja,
when wasn't I all ears whenever you made up your mind
to tell me stories of your Christian heroes? Didn't I
always applaud their noble deeds with the greatest admiration? Haven't I always wept bitter tears at their
martyrs' deaths? I must confess, however, their faith
never appeared to me the most heroic part of them.
Certainly, far more welcome to me is the doctrine that
devotion and piety towards God cannot depend upon our
fancies about God. This, as you know, dear Daja, is
what my father often said, and you agreed with him
that it is true. Why, then, are you now trying to
undermine what you've both built up so strongly in my
soul? You know, of course, my dear, such talk upsets
me when I'm getting ready for the meeting with our
friend. But, then, who knows? For me, perhaps, it's
fitting, for to me so much depends on ... But, listen,
Daja! Someone's knocking at the gate! Do you suppose
he's here at last to visit us?

                        Scene ii

[RECHA, DAJA and the TEMPLAR, for whom someone outside
opens the door with the words: Come in, Sir Knight!]

    RECHA. (Starts back, composes herself, and gets

ready to fall before him at his feet.) Yes, yes, he's
here! It *is* my rescuer!

TEMPLAR. It was precisely to escape this scene
that I delayed my coming, and yet ...

RECHA. I'm kneeling at this proud man's feet to
thank my God alone and not this man. The man refuses
to accept my thanks and wants it just as little as the
water-pail which was so active at the fire, filling
itself and pouring out its contents on the flames, and
filling up again. For all other things it didn't care
a pin! This man's the same, for, like the pail, he
too was thrown indifferently on the flames and there
I chanced to fall into his arms! It just so happened
that by chance I stayed there — like a spark upon his
mantle — lying in his arms! Then something — I
don't know what — flung both of us out of the burning
house. What reason, therefore, is there here for
thanks? In Europe, I well know, wine will spur men on
to deeds, braver by far than this one. And then, of
course, TEMPLARS must always stand ready to perform
such routine deeds! They must, as is well-known, like
hounds — only better trained — snatch people from
the water or the fire.

TEMPLAR. (After listening to her, surprised and
disturbed.) O, Daja, Daja! If in unguarded moments
my sharp tongue has ever treated you unkindly, why repeat to her every folly that escaped my lips? That
was too great a revenge! Ah, Daja! From now on when
you talk to her, I hope you'll paint me in much
brighter colors!

DAJA. To tell the truth, good sir, I'm sure those
little darts with which you pricked her heart did
little damage there as far as you're concerned!

RECHA. You say you were in trouble? You were
more worried about your troubles than about your life?

TEMPLAR. My dear, sweet child! — My whole
soul's here divided in looking and in listening! I
can't believe that this is the same girl! No, no,
she's not the one I rescued from the fire! Why, anyone who knew her would have done the same! For such
a girl who would have waited for *me* to come along?
But then, of course, disguised and terrified ... (He
pauses, gazing at Recha, and seems to be lost in
thought.)

RECHA. You're not changed — I find you're still
the same. (She pauses here before continuing to snap
him out of his astonished gaze.) But tell us, please,
good Templar, where you've been so long. In fact, I
almost feel inclined to ask — where are you now?

TEMPLAR. I'm now, my dear young lady, where I've
perhaps no right to be.

RECHA. Where you've been, you had perhaps no right
to be? That's not good!

TEMPLAR. On — on — what's the name of the mountain? Oh, yes, on Mount Sinai!

RECHA. Ah, I see, on Sinai! Very good! Now I'll
learn at last from one who really knows whether it is
true ...

TEMPLAR. What would you like to know? Whether
it's really true that the very spot can still be seen,
where Moses stood with God when ...

RECHA. No, that's not it. Wherever he stood, it
was before the Lord. That's all I need to know. But

what I'd like to verify is this: Is it really true
what people say that it's much less difficult to go up
this mountain than to come down again? For, you see,
all the hills I've climbed, I've found the opposite to
be true. But tell me, sir, why are you turning away?
Don't you want to look at me?

TEMPLAR. I'm turning away from looking at you
merely to hear you better.

RECHA. More likely so that I won't see you when
you laugh at my simplicity or when you smile at the
silly question I've just now asked about this holiest
of the holy hills. That's why you're turning away,
now isn't it?

TEMPLAR. Why, now I'll have to look into your
eyes again! Oh, I see, so now you're shutting them
tight! Who's holding back her laughter now? Why must
I try to read in the enigmatical expression of your
face what my ears tell me already — plainly, audibly?
You speak — but now you're silent? Ah, Recha, he
really spoke the truth when he said to me: "Just wait
until you know her!"

RECHA. Oh, no! Who told you that?

TEMPLAR. "Just wait until you know her," that's
what your father said to me when he talked of you.

DAJA. Don't forget me? Didn't I say that too?

TEMPLAR. But he — where is he now? Tell me,
Recha, where is your father? Can he still be with the
Sultan?

RECHA. No doubt, that's where he is.

TEMPLAR. Still with the Sultan? Oh, how could I
forget? No, he can't still be there. Down by the
cloister wall he's waiting for me! That's what we
settled on before we parted. So, please excuse me, I
must hurry off to bring him ...

DAJA. Please stay, that's what I'm here for! I'll
bring him here at once ...

TEMPLAR. No, no, don't do that! He's waiting
there for me, not you. And, who can tell, there's always the possibility, you know, that he's had a dis-
agreement with the Sultan. You don't know the Sultan!
Nathan may be in danger if I don't go!

RECHA. How can that be?

TEMPLAR. I'm telling you there's danger — danger
for me, for you, for him — if I don't get to him as
fast as possible!

Scene iii

[RECHA and DAJA]

RECHA. What can all this mean, Daja? Suddenly
he's gone! I wonder why? What's come over him?
What's driving him to my father?

DAJA. Be patient, Recha, let him go! I think
it's probably a good sign.

RECHA. A good sign of what?

DAJA. Something's happening inside him. Something's boiling, which mustn't yet boil over. Just leave him be, it's your turn now!

RECHA. My turn, Daja? It's getting so that I don't understand you any more than I do him.

DAJA. Soon you'll pay him back for all the worry that he's caused you. Don't be too hard on him or too revengeful.

RECHA. I hope you know what you're talking about, for, I assure you, I don't.

DAJA. Are you quite calm again so soon? Your old self once again?

RECHA. Yes, I am. That I am ...

DAJA. Well, you'll admit, I'm sure, your worry over him gives you more joy than pain and that you've got to thank the unrest that he's caused you for the calm you're now enjoying.

RECHA. Well, let me tell you, Daja, if I'm enjoying calm, I'm not aware of it. The only thing I can confess to you is that I'm very much surprised myself how such a calm within me can follow in the wake of such a storm. Seeing him so close and listening to him talk and to his tone of voice have — have ...

DAJA. ... left you fully satisfied, I suppose?

RECHA. No, that's not quite true! I won't go as far as that! I'm still a long way from that!

DAJA. But surely you'll admit he's satisfied your first great hunger!

RECHA. Well, yes, that's true, when you put it
that way! If that's the way you want it!

DAJA. The way *I* want it? I don't mean that at
all!

RECHA. As far as I'm concerned, he'll constantly
grow dearer as the days pass by, even if my pulse
won't wildly race at the mere mention of his name! Or
if my heart beats faster, stronger, when I think of
him! What nonsense am I prattling? Come, Daja,
please let's go just once more to the window which
overlooks the palms.

DAJA. Aha, just as I thought! It's plain to see
your first great hunger's not quite satisfied yet!

RECHA. Well, anyhow, at least I'll see the palms
again, not only him among them.

DAJA. I'll bet this chill of yours begins another
fever!

RECHA. Chill? What chill? I don't feel any
chill! And, to tell the truth, I'm very glad to see
what I see now when I am calm!

                        Scene iv

[An audience chamber in Saladin's palace. SALADIN and
SITTAH]

SALADIN. (Enters, speaking in the direction of the
door.) As soon as the Jew arrives, have him come in
here. He's certainly not in any hurry to get here.

SITTAH. Perhaps your messenger couldn't find him
right away. Perhaps he's even gone abroad!

SALADIN. O, sister! Sister, please!

SITTAH. Why, Saladin, you act as though a battle
were in question!

SALADIN. Yes, Sittah! That's exactly what I'm
doing! Preparing for a battle with weapons I'm not
sure that I can handle. I'll have to bluff and be on
my guard! I'll have to try to trap him, keep him off
his guard to have smooth sailing! When did I use such
methods? When did I resort to trickery such as this?
But now I'll have to act out this farce I've planned
and — in the end — what for, I ask? To fish for
money! Money! To extort by fear the money from a Jew!
Alas, to think that to such meanness I'm reduced to
gain for my own person the meanest of mean things!

SITTAH. The meanest thing, when it's despised too
much, dear brother, will take its own revenge.

SALADIN. Alas, that's all too true! Now let's
suppose this Jew of ours is that rare good man, so
wise and so humane, as the dervish once painted him
to you! What then?

SITTAH. If that's the way he really is, why, then
we haven't any need to trap him. A trap is needed
only for the fearful, cautious, greedy Jew! The good
and wise Jew's ours already from the start without a
trap! But still there's quite a treat in store for
you just to hear what such a man will say. Either
he'll blow his top or else with cunning evasions he'll
avoid the trap you've set for him. O, Saladin, you
can look forward to a rare treat indeed!

SALADIN. You're right, and I'm looking forward to
it with the greatest of pleasure as a rare new pastime!

SITTAH. Well, then, what else can bother you?
This Nathan's merely one of the great masses, merely a
Jew like any other Jew. Wouldn't you feel ashamed to
have him think that you're no different from what he
thinks all men to be? The better man, the man who's
more humane, but yet the greater fool — that's what
he thinks, no doubt!

SALADIN. I take it that you mean I must be wicked
so that the wicked won't think wickedly of me!

SITTAH. Of course, I do! That is, if by wickedness you mean treating our fellow-men as they deserve!

SALADIN. Whatever scheme a woman hatches, she'll
always fit it with a fine disguise. I merely need to
touch such fragile wares and they'll break to bits in
my clumsy hand. Whoever invents such schemes as that
must see them through right to the end with skillful
maneuvering and sly inventiveness. But be that as it
may! I'll dance as best I can — and think I'd rather
do it badly than well.

SITTAH. Don't think so poorly of yourself! You'll
win, if you'll only make up your mind to win! As long
as I remember, men like yourself have been trying to
convince us that the sword alone produces victory. The
lion hunting with the fox was, no doubt, ashamed of
his companion, not his cunning ...[1]

SALADIN. Women get such pleasure pulling men down

---

[1] Lessing is also well-known in German literature for his fables and
for his *Treatise on the Fable* as a literary genre.

to their level! Go, Sittah, go! I've learned my les-
son well!

    SITTAH. O, brother, must I go?

    SALADIN. Surely you don't want to stay?

    SITTAH. If not here with you, then in the ante-
chamber ...

    SALADIN. To eavesdrop on our talk? No, Sittah,
this time I must insist! Leave us alone! Go! The
curtain's rustling, so he's here. I'll see to it you
won't have long to wait. (While Sittah leaves by one
door, Nathan enters by the other. Saladin sits down.)

Scene v

[SALADIN and NATHAN]

    SALADIN. Come here, Jew! Come here to me! Come
even closer — and have no fear of me!

    NATHAN. May only your enemies fear you!

    SALADIN. Your name, I'm told, is Nathan?

    NATHAN. Yes.

    SALADIN. Nathan the Wise?

    NATHAN. No.

    SALADIN. Not by yourself, of course, but by the
people.

NATHAN. That may be — by the people!

SALADIN. Well, surely you don't think I look down
with scorn upon the judgment of the people? For a
long time now I've wanted to meet the man they call
the Wise.

NATHAN. What if they named him that in mockery?
What if *wise* means nothing more than *prudent* to the
people? And what if *purdent* simply means to figure
things out cleverly to one's own advantage?

SALADIN. You mean, I suppose, to his real advantage, his own true benefit?

NATHAN. Why, then, of course, it follows that the
selfish man would likewise be the most *prudent* man!
Then, obviously, *wise* and *prudent* would mean the same.

SALADIN. Now you're trying to prove, what you'd
like to contradict! The people, of course, don't know
men's true advantages. You, Nathan, know them, or at
least you've tried to know them. You've weighed them
and you've pondered them — and this, of course, already makes a man a *wise* man.

NATHAN. Which every man alive considers himself
to be!

SALADIN. You're far too modest! Too much modesty,
when one expects dry reason, can make a person sick.
(He leaps up.) Let's get down to business! But let's
be upright, Jew! Let's be honest!

NATHAN. I'll serve you, Saladin, in such a manner
that you'll think me worthy of serving you constantly.

SALADIN. You'll serve me? How?

NATHAN. The best of all I have I'm placing at
your service and at the lowest price.

SALADIN. What are you talking about? Surely not
your merchandise? My sister Sittah loves to bargain
and to haggle. (That's for the listener!) But I've
no use for merchants and their wares.

NATHAN. Then, no doubt, you want to know what I
happened to see on my journey or perhaps what I noticed
regarding your enemies and their strength — if openly ...

SALADIN. I don't need to ask you about that
either. I have all necessary knowledge of those
things already. In short —

NATHAN. Command me, Sultan!

SALADIN. I want your view in quite another matter, in which you'll use your wisdom. Nathan, since
you're wise, tell me as you'd tell a friend, what
faith and what law do you hold to be the best?

NATHAN. But, Sultan, I'm a Jew —

SALADIN. And I'm a Moslem! The Christian stands
between us. Only one of these three faiths can be
the true one. A man like you won't let the accident
of birth hold him to one religion! Or, if it holds
him, it will surely be of his own choice because his
insight and his reason prompt him to make that choice
as the best religion of the three. Well, then, Nathan,
let me share your insight! Let me hear *your* moving
reasons, since I've not had the time to ponder this
great question for myself. Tell me — in confidence,
of course, — the choice you've made and the reasons
for your choice. I'll also make it mine! But what's

this I see? You're startled and you're eyeing me with
suspicion. It may well be that I'm the first of all
the Sultans to have a whim like this, but yet I think
it's no unworthy whim, even for a Sultan. Don't you
agree? Well, then, speak up! Let's hear your answer!
Or, perhaps you'd like a moment to ponder your answer
to my question? Good, I grant it — (Aside) I wonder
if she's listened? I'll go look for her and have her
tell me how I've managed. (Loud) Think now, Nathan!
Think it out quickly! I'll be back in a moment.

(Enters the ante-chamber to which Sittah has gone.)

Scene vi

[NATHAN, alone]

   NATHAN. Well, now! This is indeed a ticklish
situation! What should I do now? What does the Sultan really want? I came prepared to loan him money
and he asks for TRUTH! If that weren't enough already,
he also wants it paid in ready cash, as if TRUTH were
common coinage! Now if it were old coinage, valued ·
by its weight, my task might still be fairly easy to
fulfill. But such newly-minted coins which owe their
value to the die that casts them must be counted with
the utmost care. Can any man sweep TRUTH into his
head like money swept into a sack? Who really is the
Jew here, I or the Sultan? May he not perhaps even
ask for the TRUTH in TRUTH? It's a mean thought even
to suspect he's using TRUTH merely as a snare to trap
me. But is it really mean of me to think this way?
What's too mean for great men to employ for their own
ends? I fear it's all too true. See how he breaks
the gate down, how he storms the fortress! Surely one
knocks and listens first, when one comes as a friend!

So, I'll be on my guard and watch my step. But how
must I proceed in this? To act the *common* Jew here,
that won't do at all, and still less not to act the
Jew at all. For if I don't profess to be a Jew at all,
then he'll quite likely ask: Why, in that case, aren't
you a Mussulman? Ah, yes, I've hit upon it now! I've
thought of something that will save me! Men as well
as children can be fed with fables. Ah, here he comes!
Well, let him come, I'm ready!

Scene vii

[SALADIN and NATHAN]

   SALADIN. (All is in order now, the field is clear.)
I hope I've not come back too soon and that you've
ended your deliberation. Come, then, speak up! Not a
soul hears us.

   NATHAN. As far as I'm concerned, the whole world
may listen to my words. I bid them welcome!

   SALADIN. Nathan's so confident of his cause? Well,
now, that's what I call a *wise* man! A man who never
shirks the *TRUTH*, but stakes his all upon it — his
body, life, and soul ...

   NATHAN. That's so, good Saladin, when it's need-
ful and in order.

   SALADIN. From this time onward, I can justly hope
to wear a title which I bear: *Reformer of the World
and of the Law*.

   NATHAN. That's a lovely title, I agree! But,

Sultan, before I trust myself to your hands, will you
perhaps let me tell you an old story?[2]

SALADIN. Why not? Since I was a child, I've always loved a tale well told.

NATHAN. Oh, I see, *well told*! I fear that's more
than I can claim.

SALADIN. Now why are you again so proud and yet
so modest? Come, come, let's hear your tale!

NATHAN. Many years ago there lived a man in a far
Eastern land who from the hand of his loved one had
received a ring of priceless value. It was an opal
which shed a hundred gorgeous shimmers and had a magic
power. Whoever wore this ring, believing in its power,
found grace with God and with man as well. It was no
wonder, therefore, that this Eastern man kept it always on his finger and made sure it would stay in his
own household for all time. To that son whom he loved
best of all his sons he bequeathed this ring and set
up a plan that this son should in turn bequeath it to
the son that he loved best. From that time onward,
the best-loved son, generation after generation, without respect of birth should always be the head of this
house by right of the ring alone. Do you follow me,
Sultan?

SALADIN. Yes, I understand. Go on! Go on!

NATHAN. Well now, this magic ring, handed down
from best-loved son to best-loved son for many genera-

---

[2] See the *Appendix* for a full account of the history of this "old
story." The title is, of course, *The Parable of the Rings*, made
famous by Lessing here in his *Nathan the Wise*.

tions, came at last into a father's hands, who had
three sons. All three were equally dutiful to him,
so that consequently he loved all three alike. At
various times, now this one, now that one, now the
third, when alone with him — his brothers not being
present to share the father's great love for all
three — appeared most worthy of the ring. Then,
piosly weak, he promised it to each of his beloved
sons. So things went on for quite a while, but when
the father's hour of death was drawing near, suddenly the good man became perplexed. He grieved to
think that two sons of his, trusting his word, would
be deceived and hurt. What was he to do? Quickly
he sent for a master jeweller, requesting him to make
two other rings precisely on the model of his ring.
He instructed the jeweller to spare neither cost nor
pains to make these rings identical in every way, and
this the latter did. When the three rings were
brought to him, even the father could scarcely tell
which was his own original ring. Then, full of joy,
he called each son to him in turn and gave to each his
individual blessing and his ring. Then he died. Do
you still follow me, Sultan?

SALADIN. (Who has turned away perplexed) I'm
listening, I'm listening! But quickly finish this
tale of yours! Is it over?

NATHAN. The tale's now finished. What's still to
follow anyone can guess. The father was scarcely dead
when each son came forth and showed his ring. Each
claimed to be the favored son and now the family's
head. All their searching, striving, arguing was in
vain. They couldn't prove which ring was the true
original ring, nor was this possible, ... (He pauses,
waiting for Saladin's reply.) ... anymore so than now
we can prove which religion is the true one.

SALADIN. What do you mean? Is this your answer
to my question?

NATHAN. Oh, no, it's merely my excuse that I don't
trust myself or my ability to distinguish infallibly
between the rings the father had expressly made so that
they couldn't be distinguished by any test.

SALADIN. What? The rings! You're toying with me
now! In my opinion, the religions which I named can
plainly and easily be distinguished, right down to
clothing, food, and drink!

NATHAN. What you say is true, but that's not so in
questions of their origin. As you know, all base
their creeds on history, either written down or handed
down by word of mouth. And history, you'll agree,
must be received in faith and faith alone. Well,
then, on whom do we place this implicit faith, with
never any doubt about it? Why, surely on our parents,
those from whose blood we spring! On those who daily,
hourly, gave us proofs of love from our earliest childhood on. On those who've never deceived us except
when it was better and safer for us to be deceived.
Well, then, I ask you, should I have less faith in my
forefathers than you in yours? Or, conversely, can I
demand that you must deny yours that mine may not be
contradicted? The same holds true for Christians too.
Don't you agree?

SALADIN. (Aside) By Heaven, the man is right! I
can't deny his words!

NATHAN. Now let's come back again to our three
rings. The sons appealed to law and each swore before
the judge that he directly from his father's hand had
received his ring, which was quite true. For a long
time he had his father's certain promise some day to

enjoy the privileges of his ring, and this was also
true. Each son exclaimed his father could not deceive him and — rather than let suspicion stain the
father's memory — much as he'd like to think of them
in a good light, he must believe his brothers did him
wrong. He'd soon expose the traitors and justify his
claim.

SALADIN. And now, it was up to the judge! I
can't wait to hear what he had to say. What was his
verdict in this case?

NATHAN. These were the judge's words: Bring the
father here before me as a witness. I'll hear his
testimony. If you can't do that, then leave this
court of law. I ask you, do you think this court has
been set up for solving riddles? Do you expect the
true ring will open up its mouth and of its own accord
proclaim itself? But — wait a moment! Haven't I
heard the true ring has the magic power to bring both
love and grace with God and man to its possessor?
That's the deciding point, for the two false rings
cannot have this virtue. Now, then, let's hear which
one of you loves his two brothers best. Come, come,
speak up! What? All three of you are silent? The
ring's effect, I fear, goes backward but not outward!
If that's the case, that each son loves himself the
most, why then I judge all three of you as traitors
and as betrayed as well! The three rings you now have
are false. Your father likely lost the genuine ring
and, in order to replace it and to hide his loss, had
three rings made instead.

SALADIN. O, Nathan, that is splendid! Splendid!

NATHAN. Continuing, the judge then said: Don't
seek my counsel, but here you have my verdict! Go,
each of you, be content to look upon the matter exactly

as it is. If — as you claim — each one of you received his ring from his good father's hand, then —
naturally — each one of you believes his ring to be
the true ring. It's possible, you know, your father
wouldn't any longer let one ring exert such tyranny in
his house. It's obvious enough he loved all three of
you and each one equally. He couldn't bring himself
to injure two and favor one. Now, then, let each son
strive with all his might to demonstrate his love de-
void of selfishness! Let each son vie with his two
brothers to bring to light the promised virtue of the
ring he wears upon his finger! Let each son always
nourish this great virtue to shine forth through
gentleness, a loving spirit, deeds of kindness, and
a most fervent piety and devotion to his God! Then,
in days to come, when the magic powers contained
within these rings, worn by your children's children,
will brighten up the world, I'll call you once again
before this seat of judgment after a thousand thousand
years have passed. On that day a wiser man will sit
upon it and hand down his decision. And now, depart!
So spoke the modest judge.

SALADIN. O, God! O, God!

NATHAN. Saladin, if you feel that you may be this
wiser, promised man —

SALADIN. (He hastens toward Nathan, seizes his
hand, and doesn't release it to the end of the scene.)
I should dare that? I, nothing? O, God!

NATHAN. Saladin, how do you feel about the judge's
words?

SALADIN. Good, Nathan! The thousand thousand
years of your great judge are not yet at an end. I'm
not the man to sit upon His judgment seat! Go, Nathan,
go! But always be my friend!

NATHAN. Has Saladin nothing more to ask of me?

SALADIN. Nothing, Nathan, nothing!

NATHAN. Nothing?

SALADIN. No, nothing at all — but, tell me, why do you ask this?

NATHAN. I want an opportunity to ask you for a favor.

SALADIN. Surely, you know that you don't need an opportunity to ask that! Speak up, my friend, speak up!

NATHAN. As you probably know, I've just now come home from a long journey, on which my task was to collect the debts that people owed me. I've almost too much ready cash on hand for safety. The times begin to look as if a storm is brewing. In short, I scarcely know a safe place to invest it. Now I can guess what great demands this coming war will make on you, and so I've been wondering whether you perhaps could use a portion of it.

SALADIN. (Looking him straight in the eye) O, Nathan, Nathan! I won't ask whether you've spoken with Al-Hafi before this meeting! Nor do you need to say whether a suspicion prompts you to make this offer of your own accord, your own free will ...

NATHAN. A suspicion? What do you mean?

SALADIN. Yes, Nathan, I deserve it. Please, pardon me, what else can I say? I must confess, I had made up my mind ...

NATHAN. O, Saladin, surely not to make the same
request of me!

SALADIN. Yes, it's true!

NATHAN. Then we'll both be helped! But the Templar's the cause that I can't send you all my means.
I'm sure you know him. Before all else I've got a
heavy obligation to him which I must meet.

SALADIN. What's this I hear? A Templar? Surely
you won't help my worst enemies with your good gold?

NATHAN. I'm speaking now of one man only, the man
whose life you spared.

SALADIN. Ah, yes, now you're reminding me of
something strange — most strange! I'd forgotten all
about the lad! So you know him? Where does he live?

NATHAN. Where he lives? Don't you know, Saladin,
what a great blessing fell to my lot because you
spared his life? At the risk of losing this new lease
on life, it was this very man who rescued my dear
daughter from my burning house.

SALADIN. He did? He did that? Yes, yes, he
looked like a man who'd do just that! My brother
would have done so too, my brother, whom he resembles
to a T! Is he still staying in the Holy City? Bring
him here to me! I've told my sister Sittah so many
things about her brother, a brother whom she never
knew, that I must show her now exactly how he looked
through this Templar, for he's in all respects his
double! Go, Nathan, bring him here! Just see how
many other good deeds flow out of one good act, born
of a simple human love! Go, Nathan, please bring him
here!

NATHAN. (Releasing Saladin's hand.) I'll go to him at once. And what about the other matter? Do you agree to it? Will you do me the favor that I ask?
(Leaves)

SALADIN. Of course I will! (Aside) Ah, if only I'd let Sittah stay to listen! I must go quickly to her! How can I tell her all I've got to tell her now?
(Leaves by the other side.)

Scene viii

[Under the palm trees, near the cloister, where the TEMPLAR waits for NATHAN]

TEMPLAR. (Walking up and down, struggling with himself, until he breaks out with these words) Well, here I am, a pawn — weary and tried! But that's all right with me! I don't want to know or see more clearly what's struggling in my soul! I don't want to foresee either what still will come to pass! One thing is clear to me, from Recha I've fled in vain, but in my plight I could do nothing else but flee! Well, I'll let come what may! The stroke fell much too quickly for me to escape its spell, although I struggled hard not to succumb. To see the woman I had little desire to see, and then — after I had seen her — to make a vow never to lose her from my sight! To make up my mind to always want to see her! But what am I talking about *making up my mind*? *To make up one's mind* implies to *plan*, to *act*, while I'm here suffering the pangs of love, not *acting*! Merely to see the girl, to love her at first sight, to feel bound to her by the strongest ties! These things were all one and the same, and they still are, as far as

I'm concerned! I'd rather die than even think it possible that I'll ever live apart from her and, wherever
after death we go, even there it would be my death not
to be with her! If that is love, then without the
slightest doubt the Christian Templar loves the Jewish
girl! Well, what's wrong with that? Here in the Holy
Land, a place that always will be *holy land* to me, I've
rid myself of many a prejudice. What will my Order
say? As a Knight Templar, naturally I'm finished. But
what of that? From that same hour when I became a
prisoner of Saladin, the Templar was already finished,
dead. The head which Saladin permitted me to keep,
was it really my old, my former head? No, no, I actually believe it's new and purged of all the lies and
nonsense they filled it with before, making it a slave
to poisonous prejudice. And, to tell the truth, I
feel it's now a better head, a head much more in keeping with my fatherland! Now it's beginning to think,
you see, just as my father must have thought in his
native land, unless the tales they tell of him are
false ... But are they really tales? Yes, yes,
they're tales all right, but tales which now seem
credible, more credible here where I run the risk of
falling where he fell! Where he *fell*? Well, I'd
rather *fall* with men than *stand* with children. Now
his example gives me confidence that he'd approve.
What other approval do I need? Nathan's? As far as
he's concerned, I'm sure that his assistance, not only
his approval, won't be lacking there. The noble Jew,
who wishes, none-the-less, to seem no more than Jew!
Ah, here he comes in haste, with gladness in his eyes!
But then, who ever came from Saladin in any other
frame of mind? Hello, there, Nathan! Here I am!

Scene ix

[NATHAN and the TEMPLAR]

NATHAN. Ah, hello, good friend! Is it you?

TEMPLAR. Your interview with Saladin, I take it,
has been long?

NATHAN. Not so very long, for on my way to him
I've been held back. Well, Curt, the man is truly
worthy of his fame, so much so that his fame's a mere
shadow of the man. But first of all I've something to
tell you that cannot wait.

TEMPLAR. What's that?

NATHAN. He'd like to talk to you and asks that
you come to him without delay. But first come with me
to my house, where I must pick up something for him.
Then we'll go to him.

TEMPLAR. No, Nathan, in my present state of mind
I'll never willingly enter your house again.

NATHAN. But you've been there already, haven't
you, while I've been gone? Come now, tell me, how do
you like Recha?

TEMPLAR. Beyond all expectation! Words can't
describe how much I like her. But I never want to see
her again unless I get your promise here and now that
I may see her always.

NATHAN. My friend, how should I interpret that?

TEMPLAR. (After a short pause, embracing Nathan)
My father! O, my father!

NATHAN. What's this I hear, young man?

TEMPLAR. Not son? O, Nathan, please!

NATHAN. My fine young friend!

TEMPLAR. Not my son? O, Nathan, please, I beg
you by the strongest and the tenderest ties of nature!
Don't let any other consideration sway you! Let it be
enough to be a man! Please don't reject me!

NATHAN. My dear, dear friend! ...

TEMPLAR. And what about *my son*? Not *my son*? Not
even then if the gratitude in your daughter's heart
has paved the way to our mutual love? Not even then
if only your approval's needed to melt and fuse two
loving hearts in one? — You're still silent, Nathan?

NATHAN. Good Templar, you not only surprise me,
you amaze me!

TEMPLAR. Surprise you, Nathan, amaze you, by
speaking out what I know to be your own secret
thoughts? Surely you'll not deny these secret hopes
of yours because I've put them into words? Why, then,
do I surprise you?

NATHAN. There's something I must know — Who was
this Curt von Stauffen you claim as father?

TEMPLAR. O, Nathan, why do you ask me that? Is
curiosity the only thing you feel at a time like this?

NATHAN. No, no, that's not the reason. Years ago,

you see, I knew a knight, a Conrad von Stauffen, very well.

TEMPLAR. And you're thinking, I suppose, my father had the same name as I.

NATHAN. Yes, I do.

TEMPLAR. And you're quite right, for I'm named after him. Curt, you see, is Conrad.

NATHAN. That may be, but this Conrad — the one I knew — couldn't be your father. He was, like you, a Templar and unmarried.

TEMPLAR. As for that, what does it matter?

NATHAN. What's that you're saying?

TEMPLAR. I say that, even so, he still might be my father.

NATHAN. Now, of course, you're joking!

TEMPLAR. And you, Nathan, you're taking this whole matter much too seriously! Suppose it's true, what of it? Suppose that I'm a bastard, illegitimate, perhaps? I'll grant, of course, that this wound to my pride can't be completely ignored! Well, then, absolve me of my proof of ancestry and I'll exonerate you in my turn of yours. But please don't think I'm even hinting that your family-tree could in any way be tainted! No, God forbid, not that! You could, I'm sure, unfold it leaf by leaf to Abraham and, farther back than that, I'll build it up myself and swear an oath that it's legitimate![3]

---

[3] This is, of course, ironic, since in the Bible we read of numerous cases of birth out of wedlock, even Abraham having sired an illegitimate son.

NATHAN. Now you're growing bitter and I've not
deserved it. Surely you don't think I've despised
your valor and your birth? But I'll not be offended
by your words. Let's drop the subject — there's no
more to be said!

TEMPLAR. Do you really mean it? There's no more
to be said. O, then forgive me, Nathan!

NATHAN. Come with me, my good friend, come!

TEMPLAR. First tell me where. Not to your house,
I hope? That I won't do, I can't do! There's fire
there! I'll wait for you right here, but you go there
yourself! I'll see her again only if many, many times
you'll let me see her after that. But if I don't see
her again, I've seen her far too often even now ...

NATHAN. I'll hurry back.

Scene x

[The TEMPLAR, and soon after DAJA]

TEMPLAR. I've had enough and more than enough!
The human brain is almost limitless in its grasp, but
suddenly it's often filled to bursting with a mere
trifle! But then, this really matters very little,
nothing! Let it be full of what it wants to be! Let
patience solve the problem! The spirit soon rejects
the trivial stuff and once again makes room for light
and order to return. Is this the first time that I'm
really in love? Or was what I before called love not
really love at all? Is real love only what I'm suffering now?

DAJA. (Entering from the side) O, sir! Sir!

TEMPLAR. Who's calling? Oh, Daja, it's you?

DAJA. I've slipped past him, but where you're
standing now he still might see us. Let's move behind this tree.

TEMPLAR. What's troubling you, Daja? Why so
secretive? Tell me why you're acting so perturbed!

DAJA. The reason why I'm coming to you now does,
in fact, concern a secret, an important secret. Perhaps a double secret would be more correct. The first
one only I know, the second only you can know. Let's
swap our secrets! You trust me with yours, then I'll
trust you with mine.

TEMPLAR. Gladly, Daja, but first I'd like to know
just what you think mine is. But let's hear yours
first, for out of it mine surely will emerge.

DAJA. No, no, that won't do at all! You must
tell yours first, then I'll follow you with mine. For
mine, you see, can't help you one little bit unless
you tell me yours before it. But please let's get on
with it. If I've got to drag it out of you with my
questions, then you've confided nothing. Then my
secret remains my secret and yours will be out, be
known to me. O, you poor fellow! Why do you men --
without exception — get it in your heads that you
can keep such secrets from us poor women?

TEMPLAR. I suppose that oftentimes includes
secrets we don't know we have.

DAJA. That's quite possible, yes, so I'll appoint
myself the friend to make your secret known to yourself.

Tell me, what was it made you vanish without a moment's notice in a cloud and leave your friends dumbfounded? Why aren't you returning now with Nathan to
his house? Is it perhaps that you like our Recha so
very little which makes you stay away? Is that the
reason? Or should I ask, perhaps, so very much? Tell
me, my friend, am I to see in you the fluttering of
the poor captive bird, limed to the tree? In short,
confess to me that you're in love with her, madly in
love with her, and then I'll tell you ...

TEMPLAR. Madly in love with her! O, Daja, your
insight truly is amazing.

DAJA. Just admit your *love* for Recha, I'll not
hold you to your *madness*!

TEMPLAR. It must, I suppose, be regarded as sheer
madness! A Christian Templar loving a Jewish girl!

DAJA. I must admit there doesn't seem much sense
in that — and yet, sometimes there's more sense in
things than anyone could dream of, than in our *wildest*
dreams! It's not at all improbable, you know, that
Christ can lead us to Himself by ways which — on his
own — the wisest man would never find.

TEMPLAR. Your words, good lady, are very solemn.
(Aside) Now, if Providence were used instead of Christ,
wouldn't she be right? (Loud) You're planting a
curiosity in my soul, a curiosity which I've never
felt before.

DAJA. Well, my friend, this land's the land of
miracles, you know!

TEMPLAR. (Aside) Yes, miracles! But how can it
be otherwise, since all these nations mass themselves

together here? (Loud) Very well, good lady, consider
it confessed, the thing you wish to know! Yes, I
really love her — our Recha — love her madly, and I
don't know how I'll live without her! I ...

DAJA. You really do, my friend? Then pledge your
oath to me that you'll take her for your own and save
my Recha while she lives here on earth and in the
great beyond, the afterlife, eternally.

TEMPLAR. How can I do that? How can I swear to
do what I've no right, no power, to carry out?

DAJA. But even though you're not aware of it, you
do have that right, that power. With a few simple
words, I'll give you that right, that power.

TEMPLAR. So that even her father can't object to
or obstruct this marriage?

DAJA. Her father? What father? Her father *must*
agree to it.

TEMPLAR. *Must,* Daja? Did you say *must*? He's not
fallen prey to robbers yet, you know! So there's no
such thing as *must* for him!

DAJA. What I'm telling you is true! In the end
he *must* consent, and he'll be glad to do it too!

TEMPLAR. He *must* and he'll be *glad* to do it? What
have you to say, when I now tell you that I've already
felt him out on this very matter?

DAJA. And he wouldn't agree?

TEMPLAR. No, he wouldn't! Definitely not! In
fact, so sharp and rude was his objection, that I was
deeply hurt by it!

DAJA. What are you telling me? You told him —
even if it merely was a hint — of your great love
for Recha and he didn't leap for joy? You mean to say
he coldly brushed you off and indicated difficulties?

TEMPLAR. That's exactly how it was!

DAJA. Then I'll not hesitate a single minute
longer ... (Pause)

TEMPLAR. And yet — you *are* reflecting still!

DAJA. All his other acts prove that Nathan's kind!
I'm well aware how much I owe to him myself! But in
this one thing he won't listen! He won't budge an
inch! Oh, Heaven only knows, my heart bleeds to have
to force him to his senses in this way!

TEMPLAR. I beg you, Daja, once and for all, explain this riddle to *me*! But if you're not completely
sure yourself of what you plan to tell me, whether good
or bad, shameful or laudable, then, please, say nothing. I'll forget you've got a secret which you've
left unspoken.

DAJA. No, no! It really hurts me more in this
case not to speak. Well, here goes! I'll have you
know our Recha's not a Jewess, she's a Christian!

TEMPLAR. Oh, really? Well, Daja, good for you!
Was that so hard to say? Surely you needn't shrink
from so hard a task! You most certainly must continue
in your zeal to fill heaven with Christians if you
can't do so on earth!

DAJA. What's this you're telling me? Is this the
mockery and the sarcasm my news deserves from you?
Doesn't the fact that Recha is a Christian fill your

heart with joy, you, a Christian Templar, who claims
to be in love with her?

TEMPLAR. Oh, that's for sure, especially since
she's a Christian of your making!

DAJA. So, that's what you think? Very well, then,
let's forget about it! But no, no, for I must find the
man who'll convert her back to Christianity. It's been
her great misfortune to be far too long what now she
mustn't become, a Jewess!

TEMPLAR. Explain this, Daja, or leave my sight!

DAJA. She's a Christian child, born of Christian
parents, she's baptized and ...

TEMPLAR. And what about Nathan?

DAJA. Nathan's not her father!

TEMPLAR. Nathan's not her father? O, Daja, are
you sure you know what you are saying?

DAJA. I'm telling you the truth, which many times
has cost me bitter tears. No, Nathan's not her father!

TEMPLAR. Do you mean to tell me he only brought
her up as his adopted daughter? Are you saying he had
this child, this Christian child, brought up a Jewess?

DAJA. I'm positive he did just that.

TEMPLAR. And she knows nothing of her birth? She's
never learned from him that she was born a Christian,
not a Jewess?

DAJA. Never! Never!

TEMPLAR. And he's not only brought up Recha in this delusion, but left the girl in this deception to this day?

DAJA. Yes, yes, alas, that's so!

TEMPLAR. Why, Nathan, who's so wise and good, has gone against the rights of nature here. He's stifled the thoughts in this girl's heart which — if left alone — would go quite different ways. Daja, what you've just told me is a very serious matter, involving basic issues. I'm quite perplexed, in doubt what I must do. Give me a little time to think it over, please. Go now, for he'll be coming back here any moment and might surprise us talking of these things. Therefore, Daja, go! Go!

DAJA. I'd surely die if he'd catch me here!

TEMPLAR. I can't talk calmly to him now! If by chance you meet him, tell him I'll meet him in a little while at the Sultan's palace.

DAJA. Be sure you don't let on to him what you know now. This, of course, for you now seals the matter and relieves you of all doubts and scruples when you think of Recha and her fate. If you make up your mind to take her with you when you go to Europe, I beg you don't leave me behind ...

TEMPLAR. You have my word on that, but you must leave me now! (Daja leaves.)

[END OF ACT THREE]

ACT FOUR

Scene i

[Scene: In the cloisters of the convent. The FRIAR
and soon after the TEMPLAR]

FRIAR. Well, well, of course the Patriarch's right!
Even though no chore he's placed upon my shoulders before this time has ever been successful, I wonder why
he picks such chores for me? I loathe this trickery
of his and it's not my nature to play the role of his
persuader. Nor do I want to stick my nose in everything or play the meddler for him! Really now, I ask
you, did I forsake the world to lead a life like this,
to be involved through him more and more in other people's business?

TEMPLAR. (Entering hastily) Greetings to you,
good friar! We meet again! I've been looking for you
a long time now!

FRIAR. You've been looking for me, my friend?

TEMPLAR. Why, yes! Have you forgotten me?

FRIAR. Oh no, good Templar, no, indeed! Only, I
thought I'd never get to meet you in my life again.
In fact, I prayed to our good Lord that we might never
meet again! For, you see, Heaven only knows how much
I loathed the errand I was told to bring to you before! He likewise knows how much I hoped I'd find no
one to accept that errand. He also knows how over-
joyed I was that you rejected without a moment's
thought an act which certainly was unbecoming to your

105

knighthood. I cannot tell you how very glad I really
was! But things have turned out wrong, I fear, for
now we meet again!

TEMPLAR. Apparently you know the reason why I'm
here, though I myself can scarcely guess.

FRIAR. I'm guessing too, of course. Perhaps
you've thought things over and concluded that after
all is said and done the Patriarch's quite right.
Perhaps you're looking forward to the fame and honor
his plan will bring you. Perhaps you feel a foe is
still a foe, even though seven times over he's proved
himself our angel. Perhaps with your own flesh and
blood you've taken counsel and now you come again to
offer him your service. O, my God!

TEMPLAR. No, good friar, that's not so at all!
Set your mind at ease! It's not for that I'm coming
to consult the Patriarch. My feelings on that subject are still the same as they were before. I
wouldn't want to lose for anything in the world that
respect of which a man like you — so honest, so
pious, and so kind — has thought me worthy. No
that's not it at all. I've simply come to ask the
Patriarch's advice ...

FRIAR. You — of him? You, a knight, ask a priest
for his advice? (Looking around him timidly)

TEMPLAR. Well — yes. The matter, you see, is
of a priestly nature.

FRIAR. That may be, but you'll not find a priest
asking for a knight's advice, however knightly the
matter may be!

TEMPLAR. That's true, but it's a privilege a

priest enjoys to be wrong at times, a privilege, I
might add, which no one envies him. In fact, if only
I myself were personally in question and it were up to
me alone to produce the answer, what need — I ask
you — would I have of Patriarchs? But, as for certain matters, I'd rather do them not so well on the
advice of others than do them very well by my own
will. Besides, I'm quite aware that religion very
definitely means party and whoever thinks himself no
partisan in this, that man unconsciously defends his
favored faith. Since this is so, it's right that I
should take this step.

     FRIAR. I'll not answer that, for I'm not sure at
all if I understand you right, my friend.

     TEMPLAR. (Aside) Well, now! Let's see, what do
I really want? Decree or counsel? Plain advice or
refined evasion? (Loud) I thank you, friar, for your
words of wisdom. But why consult the Patriarch? You,
good friar, be my Patriarch! I'd much rather ask the
Christian under the Patriarch than the Patriarch as a
Christian. Well, then, here's my question — my problem is ...

     FRIAR. Say no more, good Templar, please stop
right there! What good can come of this? My dear man,
you're quite wrong about me, you know! The man who
knows too much, merely has more worry! As far as I'm
concerned, one worry is enough for me, more than
enough, in fact! Oh, good! Look over there comes the
very man you need, the Patriarch, to relieve me in
this awkward plight of mine! So, just stay where you
are, for he's already seen you!

Scene ii

[The PATRIARCH, approaching with priestly pomp by way
of the one cloister, and the former two, the FRIAR and
the TEMPLAR]

TEMPLAR. I wish I could avoid him! He's not at
all the kind of man I want to talk to! A portly,
rosy-cheeked, and cheery churchman! Behold the splendor of the man!

FRIAR. Oh, this is nothing, nothing at all! You
should just see him on his way to court! He's coming
from a sick man now.

TEMPLAR. How inferior Saladin must feel in this
man's presence!

PATRIARCH. (Approaching, signals to the Friar)
Well now, that's our Templar, I suppose? What does he
want?

FRIAR. That I don't know.

PATRIARCH. (Approaching the Templar, while the
Friar and his retinue retire) Well, well, good Templar! I'm very, very glad indeed to see you, brave
young man. Why, you're still a mere lad! Well now,
with God's help, you may develop into something great.

TEMPLAR. I fear, your reverence, no more than
what's already there, perhaps less.

PATRIARCH. At least I hope a pious knight like
you may prosper many years for the good and glory of
all Christendom and God's own cause! This will, I'm

sure, not fail, if you, brave youth, will listen to
the mature wisdom of age — as, of course, it should.
How can I serve you now, my friend?

TEMPLAR. By giving me good counsel, which youth
lacks.

PATRIARCH. Very willingly, if youth will only
take my counsel.

TEMPLAR. Yes, of course, but yet not blindly.

PATRIARCH. Naturally not! Who could expect you
to do that? No, no one should ever be asked not to
use his reason, his God-given reason, in its proper
place. But let me emphasize *its proper place,* not
everywhere! Oh, no, not everywhere! Now suppose, for
instance, that God wills through one of His good
angels — that is, through a servant of His Word —
to suggest a way to us, by which we'll further and
establish the welfare and prosperity of all Christendom and His great Church in some uncommon means of
action. I ask you, who'll dare to question in a case
like that, by mere reason, Almighty God's decree,
who's created reason? Who'll dare put to the test
the eternal law of the glory of the Heavens according
to the insignificant rules which vain men now call
reason? But come, enough of this! What's the problem, sir, for which you need my counsel?

TEMPLAR. Just this, most reverent father: Let's
suppose a Jew has in his house an only child, a young
girl. He's raised this girl not only with the greatest care, but also with the greatest kindness. Besides, he's loved her as he loves his precious soul
and she's returned his love most piously. Now, let's
suppose too, that rumor had it that this girl wasn't
really the daughter of the Jew at all. He'd chosen

her when still an infant for his own and, whether he
bought or stole her, no matter, he'd brought her to
his home. But this girl — as was later learned —
was born of Christian parents and had been baptized
too. The Jew had only raised her as a Jewess and let
her think herself a Jewess and his true daughter. I
ask you now, most reverent father, what must be done
in such a situation?

  PATRIARCH. I shudder at the thought! But, sir,
first you must tell me whether this case of yours is
merely fiction or whether it's indeed a fact. What I
mean is this: Have you, sir, merely imagined this
whole story or has it really happened and is it happening now?

  TEMPLAR. I didn't think that mattered. I merely
wished to find out your opinion, reverent father.

  PATRIARCH. You didn't think that mattered! O,
sir, here you see how greatly the arrogant human mind
can be mistaken in spiritual matters such as this!
No, no, sir, please let me explain. Now, if this case
which you've put before me is just a figment of your
fancy, why then it's not even worth the trouble to
give serious thought to its solution. Such things are
best left to those theatres where disputations such as
this are frequently presented pro and con with great
applause by the whole audience attending. But, sir,
if, on the other hand, you've no trifles such as that
in mind, fit only for the stage, if what you've said
is fact and happening here within my diocese, yes even
in this very city of Jerusalem, why, then ...

  TEMPLAR. What then, most reverent father?

  PATRIARCH. Then, without a single day's delay,
the Jew in question must submit to the full penalty

which both the papal and the imperial laws provide for such an outrage, such a wicked crime!

TEMPLAR. O, reverent father, what is this penalty you speak of?

PATRIARCH. The laws I've mentioned provide the stake, the fire, for any Jew who leads a Christian to apostasy ...

TEMPLAR. What? Do you mean the terrible flame?

PATRIARCH. Why, yes! And just imagine how much more severe the penalty will be for such a wicked Jew who's snatched up by force a poor Christian girl from the sacred bond of baptism! Tell me, now, isn't all we do to children really cruel? You understand, of course, by that I mean all excepting what the Church may do to children!

TEMPLAR. But suppose the child had starved to death or died in abject poverty, if the Jew in question hadn't shown compassion. What then?

PATRIARCH. That matters not a bit! Why should it make a difference? The Jew must burn, I tell you! You see, it would have been far better if the girl had died in utter misery than be saved this way to the eternal damnation of her soul. I ask you, by what right does a Jew dare to forestall God Almighty? For, obviously, God can save anyone He wants to save without the interference of this Jew!

TEMPLAR. Yes, I agree, and also, I imagine, in spite of such a Jew!

PATRIARCH. That matters not a bit! The Jew must burn!

TEMPLAR. That touches me to the heart! Especially when it's rumored he's not brought up this girl in
his own Jewish faith so much as in no faith at all.
It's claimed he's taught her no more no less concerning God than satisfies her reason.

PATRIARCH. That matters nothing either! The Jew
must burn! In fact, on this one count alone he's condemned himself to burn a dozen times. Just imagine!
To let a child grow up without a faith! Imagine! To
be so remiss in duty not to teach a fervent love for
God to this dear child! What greater wickedness can
there be? I really wonder, good Templar, that you
yourself haven't ...

TEMPLAR. Whatever must be done, most reverent
father, if God will, I leave to the confessional ...
                          (He starts to leave.)

PATRIARCH. What? You'll not tell me even now?
This criminal Jew, you'll still leave him unnamed?
You'll not bring him to me here and now? Well, so be
it, I think I know the way to go about it! I'll go
directly to the Sultan. Because of his sworn capitu-
lation which bears his seal, Saladin's duty-bound to
protect us in all rights and rules pertaining to our
Holy Faith and our Christian Church. Praise be to
God! We have the original, not a copy! We have his
hand and seal! Yes, it's in our hands! It won't be
hard to make him understand how dangerous it's to his
state when one believes in nothing! Why, every civil
bond is ripped apart when men are bold enough to dare
to have no faith! We must get rid of such an outrage!

TEMPLAR. It really is a pity, most reverent
father, that I can't stay here any longer to enjoy
your words of wisdom. You must excuse me, for I've
been asked to come to Saladin's palace.

PATRIARCH. Oh, really?   Well, now ... in that
case ...

TEMPLAR. Yes, of course, I'll prepare him for
your visit, if that's your wish, most reverent father.

PATRIARCH. Ah, yes! ... Ah! ... I know, good
Templar, you've gained the Sultan's highest favor!
Please remember me to him and tell him I'm always at
his service. In all my acts, remind him, that I'm
driven purely by my zeal for God and if perchance I
sometimes carry matters to excess, it's for Him and
Him alone that I do these things! But, my friend,
surely there's no need now to keep the truth from me.
Tell me it's not true, that case about the Jew, the
tale that you've just told me. You've just been testing me, now haven't you? I mean to say ...

TEMPLAR. Yes, testing you.   (Leaves)

PATRIARCH. Well, just the same, I'll dig much
deeper until I get down to the very bottom of this
matter. But that's really another chore for Brother
Bonafides! Here, my son!

(While speaking, he leaves to seek the Friar.)

Scene iii

[Scene: A chamber in Saladin's palace, into which a
number of sacks are being carried by slaves and placed
side by side on the floor. SALADIN and soon after
SITTAH]

SALADIN. (Entering) Well, now, there seems to be
no end to this gold! Is there still much to come?

SLAVE. At least as much again.

SALADIN. Take the rest to Sittah. Where's Al-
Hafi? Let him take charge of these sacks right away!
Or, should I send them to the old man's stronghold in
the mountains? If I keep them here, the gold will
merely slip like water through my fingers. But, then,
of course, a person does grow hard at last. I tell
you, it will take some cunning to get a single penny
out of me! At least until the money out of Egypt arrives here safely, the poor must find their bread some
other place. At the Holy Sepulchre I must provide the
alms as I've done before. These must go on, or else
all Christian pilgrims will leave with empty hands.
If only I could ...

SITTAH. What's this all about? What's all this
money doing here with me?

SALADIN. I'm merely paying up my debts to you.
What's over you can use for other needs.

SITTAH. Hasn't old Nathan come back yet with his
friend, the Templar?

SALADIN. He's looking for him everywhere.

SITTAH. Look what I've found when going through
my trinkets.   (Shows him a small picture.)

SALADIN. Why, it's my brother! That's who it is,
my brother! Was my brother, *was*, alas! That's the
brave young hero I lost so soon! O, dear brother, if
only you had been constantly at my side since you
passed away, what couldn't I have done! Give me the
picture, Sittah, for, you see, I remember it very
clearly. He gave it to your older sister, Lilla, one
morning when holding him close she wouldn't let him

go. That was the last day he rode out alone mounted
on his horse. And I, I let him ride alone, alas!
Your sister, Lilla, died of grief when he failed to
return. She never forgave me that I let him ride
away alone! Since that day he disappeared completely! We've never had the joy of seeing him again!

SITTAH. O, Saladin, my poor brother!

SALADIN. Let's talk no more of that! God's will
be done! There will come a day when we'll all ride
out and not come back again! Besides — who knows?
It's not death alone that frustrates all our plans.
Your brother also had his enemies and it's a well-
known fact that very often the strongest man falls
just as soon as does the weakest. As far as he's concerned, let that be as it may! But, as for me, I must
compare the picture with this Templar, for then perhaps I'll see how much my fancy has deceived me.

SITTAH. That's the reason why I brought it here.
But let me keep it just the same! A woman, you know,
can make any fine distinctions better than a man.

SALADIN. (To an usher who enters) Speak up!
Who's there? The Templar? Tell him to come in!

SITTAH. I'll sit here and keep out of your way.
Nor will I let my curious looks disturb him.
        (She sits down to one side on a couch and lets her
                                        veil fall.)

SALADIN. Very well, very well! (Aside) Now let
me hear his voice! What will it tell me? I still remember clearly the tone of Assad's voice and I hope it
will awaken in this Templar.

Scene iv

[The TEMPLAR and SALADIN]

TEMPLAR. May I, Sultan, your prisoner, ...

SALADIN. My *prisoner*? When I give a person the
gift of life, don't I also give him his freedom?

TEMPLAR. What you decide to do, O, Sultan, it's
better that I hear it from your lips, rather than an-
ticipate and guess what your decision is. But, sire,
to offer special thanks to you for this life you spared
agrees neither with my nature nor with the precepts of
my Order. In any situation, it's always at your service.

SALADIN. Only one thing I ask of you, don't ever
put your life to use against me. Another pair of
hands I needn't grudge my foes, but another heart like
yours I cannot spare. Of that I'm sure, for in no respect am I deceived in you, my brave young man! You
are indeed the spitting image of my Assad both in body
and in soul — so much so, that I might almost ask you
where you've been hiding all this time? In what cave
you've slept? In what Ginnistan and by what kindly
keeper this flower has all these years been kept so
fresh? I might also ask you to recall all the things
we used to do together long ago — the woods through
which we roamed, our mounted gallops over the free and
open fields. I might, in fact, even scold you for
having kept a secret from me and gone off on an adven-
ture without taking me along. Yes, that's what I
might do if I saw only you and not myself as well!
Well, enough of that! There's so much truth remains
of this sweet dream, that in the autumn of my years my

dearest brother looms up again right here. Good Templar, won't you agree to have it so?

TEMPLAR. Yes, yes, of course! Whatever comes to me from you, anything at all, is welcome to my soul.

SALADIN. Let's try it right away! Will you live here — with me and about me? Whether it be as a Moslem or as a Christian, that matters not a bit! Dress in the white cloak or the gaberdine, in turban or in helmet, dress as you please, it's all the same to me! I've never been in favor of just one bark growing on every tree found in the woods!

TEMPLAR. Otherwise you'd hardly be what you are now, the conqueror who'd rather till his own good field by the Grace of God!

SALADIN. Well, now, good friend, if your opinion of me is as good as that, why then we're half agreed already!

TEMPLAR. No, Sultan, we're in *complete* agreement.

SALADIN. (Offering him his hand) I have your word on that?

TEMPLAR. A man's as good as his word! So, Saladin, my honor's here at stake. I give you something you'll never take from me. I'm yours completely, and I'm wholly at your service.

SALADIN. My gain is far too great for one day! Far too great, good Templar! But, tell me, didn't he come with you?

TEMPLAR. Who?

SALADIN. Your Nathan.

TEMPLAR. No, I came alone.

SALADIN. Ah, my friend, what a brave deed you performed at his burning house! And what good luck that your action turned out well for Nathan, that great man!

TEMPLAR. (Coldly) Oh, Nathan! Yes!

SALADIN. Why so cold? Don't be that way, young man! When God decides to do a good deed through us, we mustn't be so cold, nor in our modesty even appear to be that way.

TEMPLAR. In our strange world, for everything there are several points of view. It's often hard to see how they are reconciled.

SALADIN. Stick to the truth — only the truth — and praise our good Lord who knows best how to reconcile these views. But, young man, if you're as fussy as all that, why, then I'll also have to be on my guard with you. For, my good friend, you must know, that I'm a man of many moods myself, I'm sorry to say, moods which even I find hard to bring to harmony.

TEMPLAR. I'm sorry to hear that. Suspicion's not my weakness and never was, but ...

SALADIN. Well, then, tell me, who's made you suspicious now? It almost seems as if it's Nathan! But — suspect Nathan? You? Come now, you must explain yourself! You've got to tell me! What's this all about?

TEMPLAR. I've got nothing against Nathan. I'm angry only with myself.

SALADIN. But, why?

TEMPLAR. Simply because I dreamed a Jew this once
might perhaps forget to be a Jew! And I dreamed it —
you must know — when wide awake!

SALADIN. Well, now, young man, let's hear all
about your waking dream! I'm sure all this must be
merely a trifling annoyance on your part!

TEMPLAR. No, sire, it's much more than that! You
know, of course, of Nathan's daughter and what I did
for her. I did it — well — because I did! But
then — unhappily — I was too proud to see the girl
again. Day after day, disdainful, I refused to come
to her and get from her the thanks she thought my due.
Her father at the time was absent on a journey. When
he returned, he heard the story. He sought me out and
thanked me, and then expressed the hope that I'd come
to see his daughter and approve of her. He talked of
happy future days and of my prospects. Well, to make
the story short, he talked and won me over. I went to
see his daughter and found a darling such as I've ...
O, Sultan, I'm ashamed to tell you!

SALADIN. Ashamed? Ashamed! You mean, perhaps,
because a Jewish girl could touch your heart? But
that's all past, I suppose?

TEMPLAR. I'm ashamed that my impetuous heart,
kindled by Nathan's kind inviting words, resisted this
passion so feebly! I'm a wretched fool! I fell a
second time into the fire in Nathan's house! This
time I wooed the girl and now I've been rejected!

SALADIN. Rejected?

TEMPLAR. Well, her wise father didn't tell me

directly to leave his house! Oh, no, not that! Her
wise father said he must first inquire about me and
must first consider! But, then, didn't I do precisely the same thing too? Did I inquire about Nathan and
his house when it was in flames? Did I first consider
— even for a moment — when his Recha screamed in the
searing fire? Of course, I did! O, God, it's certainly a wonderful thing on Nathan's part to be so
wise, so thoughtful, and so grateful!

SALADIN. Now, now, young knight, don't be so sar-
castic! You must have patience with an old man such
as Nathan! You're still a young man, you must remember that! Tell me, how long, do you suppose, will
this refusal last? Will he perhaps demand that you
must first become a Jew?

TEMPLAR. A Jew! Who knows what he'll demand?

SALADIN. *Who knows?* Why, any man who knows the
type of man that Nathan is!

TEMPLAR. Merely because we see the defects of the
superstition we grew up in, it doesn't lose its hold
upon our souls! Those men who mock their chains are
not all free!

SALADIN. That's wisely said! But in Nathan's
case ...

TEMPLAR. The most bigoted of superstitions is to
hold one's own faith to be the only right one! ...

SALADIN. That may be, but Nathan ...

TEMPLAR. ... which poor, blind men must trust until they see the light, which light alone ...

SALADIN. Yes, I agree! But, good friend, as for
Nathan, he hasn't any weakness such as that!

TEMPLAR. I thought so too! But what if this para-
gon of yours were merely a common Jew like all the
others? What if he'd take a Christian child into his
house and bring her up a Jewess? Now what's your verdict, sire?

SALADIN. Tell me, who's slandering Nathan in this
way?

TEMPLAR. The same sweet girl he's using to decoy
me, whose love he dangles before my eyes as a hope, in
payment for her rescue which he claims that I've not
done in vain. No, Saladin, this girl is not his daughter, no, she's a Christian child, an orphan or a cast-
away.

SALADIN. And yet, in spite of that, he won't let
you have her?

TEMPLAR. (Hotly) Will he or won't he? At any
rate, his treachery is now uncovered! He's found out
— this babbler of equality and tolerance! And on the
scent of this Jewish wolf, disguising himself in the
sheep's clothing of philosophy, I'll soon put dogs to
rip the sham clothes off his back and show him as he
really is!

SALADIN. (Earnestly) Calm, Christian, calm down!
Please be calm!

TEMPLAR. What do you mean, sire, be calm, Christian! The Jew and Moslem want their own to be nothing
else but Jew and Moslem! Tell me, why is the Christian
denied to make Christians of his own?

SALADIN.   Calm down, Christian, be calm!

TEMPLAR.   (Composed)   I feel the weight of this
reproach which you cram into this one word *Christian*!
I wonder, frankly, just how your Assad would have
acted in my place?

SALADIN.   No better than you're acting now! He'd
probably act with just as much vehemence and fury!
But what I'd like to know is this: Who's taught you
so soon to pierce my armor with a single word, *Assad*,
just as he used to do? But, be that as it may, this
I know for sure: Even if these things are exactly as
you claim, they're not the things that I'll associate
with the tolerance of Nathan! I can't find in them
reason to change my good opinion of this man! He's
still my friend, and friends of mine must not be at
odds! So, what I'm saying to you now is simply this:
Go softly, cautiously! Whatever you do, don't make
Nathan a prey to the fanatics of your Christian rabble!
Don't stir up this placid pool, for if your priests
were to avenge themselves on Nathan, then I'd be duty-
bound to give him my protection! So, my advice to
you is this: Don't be a Christian who's loathed by
both Jew and Moslem!

TEMPLAR.   Soon it will be too late to avoid even
that! The fact is I'm already warned by the Patriarch's thirst for blood! He's chosen me to be his
tool in carrying out his secret plans!

SALADIN.   What's this you're saying? Don't tell
me you went to him first, not to me?

TEMPLAR.   Yes, sire, that's exactly what I did on
the spur of the moment when my mind was in a whirl!
I ask you, please, forgive me! Now, I fear, you'll
no longer see the features of your brother Assad in my
face.

SALADIN. You know, of course, it was this very
fear that hurt! But, then, I'm quite aware that
faults and virtues often dwell together in one person. Go now, my friend, go and look for Nathan, just
as he looked for you, and bring him here to me! Now
it's up to me to bring you two together! You must be
serious and calm for your sweetheart's sake, for she's
yours. It may well be Nathan understands already
that — even though he's not allowed her to eat hog's
meat while in his house — he's raised a Christian
child! Go, then, my friend, and find him!

(The Templar leaves and Sittah comes forward.)

Scene v

[SALADIN and SITTAH]

SITTAH. How strange, how very strange!

SALADIN. Isn't it, Sittah? Don't you agree my
brother Assad must have been a bright and handsome
fellow? Just look here.
(He shows her the picture.)

SITTAH. I certainly agree if he looked like this
and that our Templar must certainly have posed for
this picture! But, dear brother, why didn't you
question him about his parentage? How could you forget?

SALADIN. You're right, especially about his
mother, and, more precisely whether she ever came into
this region! What do you think?

SITTAH. You must be sure to ask him that!

SALADIN. It's certainly very likely! Assad was a
great favorite with fair Christian ladies and so devoted to them too, that once the story ran ... but no,
no! I don't want to talk of that! I'll say no more
about it! It's quite enough for me that I've got him
back again! I'll treat him as my own with all his
faults and all the love he carries in his tender heart.
This young girl that he loves, this girl in Nathan's
house, Nathan must give him as his own! What do you
think about it, Sittah?

SITTAH. Not *give* him, Saladin, *leave* him!

SALADIN. What you say is true! What right has
Nathan over her if he's not her father? Only the man
who saved her in her mortal danger from the flames can
now take over her unknown father's rights!

SITTAH. Well then, Saladin, why don't you bring
this girl directly to your palace and take her out of
her illegal Jewish father's hands?

SALADIN. Will that be really necessary, Sittah?

SITTAH. No, not really necessary. It's merely my
curiosity, I suppose, which prods me on to give you
this advice. For certain men, you see, I like to know
at once what type of girl they love.

SALADIN. Very well, then, Sittah, send for the
girl to come here right away!

SITTAH. O, my dear brother, will you really let
me do it?

SALADIN. Yes, but please spare Nathan! Nathan
must not think, not even have the slightest suspicion,
that we're taking the girl from him by force.

SITTAH. Have no fear of that! I'll see to it
that it doesn't happen!

SALADIN. I must go now to find out where Al-Hafi's
hiding.

Scene vi

[Scene: The open court in Nathan's house, opposite
the palm grove, as in Act I, Scene i. Part of the
merchandise and the jewels, of which they speak, is
now unpacked. NATHAN and DAJA]

DAJA. O, Nathan, how lovely all this is! The
richest of the rich! The choisest of the choice!
Such splendor's quite in keeping with your generosity!
Where do they make a lovely silver dress like this,
woven through with threads of gold? How great must
be its cost! O, surely it's a *wedding* dress, the
rarest *bridal* gown! A dress fit for a queen!

NATHAN. A *wedding* dress? A *bridal* gown? Why do
you call it that?

DAJA. I know, of course, you didn't think of that
when buying it. But surely, Nathan, you must agree
that's what it is and nothing else, a *wedding* dress,
as if it had been ordered for that purpose. The sil-
very ground material symbolizes innocence, and the
heavy golden threads they've woven through it are
emblems, every one of them, of riches! Don't you see?
It's lovely, lovely!

NATHAN. Why all this ecstasy, this sheer delight?
Whose wedding dress are you referring to in this way

with such great learning? Tell me, Daja, are you going to be a bride?

DAJA. I, a bride?

NATHAN. Well then, who is?

DAJA. I? Good Heavens, no!

NATHAN. Who, then? Whose wedding dress is it
that you're raving about? All this is yours and no
one else's.

DAJA. Mine? It's for me? It's not for Recha?

NATHAN. What I've brought for Recha has been unpacked elsewhere. Come, come, Daja, take your gifts.

DAJA. Nathan, even if these gorgeous gifts were
the greatest treasures in the world, I wouldn't touch
them except on one condition. First you must swear to
me that you'll accept and approve the great good fortune that Heaven has granted you and won't perhaps
grant you a second time.

NATHAN. Accept? Approve? Accept and approve
what? What great good fortune?

DAJA. O, Nathan, why pretend to be so blind?
I'll tell you bluntly! The Templar knight loves
Recha! I beg you, Nathan, give her to him! In doing
so, you'll put an end to this sin you are committing,
a sin which can't be kept a secret any longer. Then
Recha will again live among Christians and will become
once more what she was and is. And you, dear Nathan,
for all the kindness you have shown us — for which
we'll be forever grateful — you'll not have merely
heaped up coals of fire on your own head!

NATHAN. Oh, now I see it all! You're harping the
same old tune again, only this time it's fitted to a
different string! This harp of yours, alas, which
can't be silenced or kept in tune!

DAJA. What do you mean by that?

NATHAN. I like your Templar very much and I'd
rather give my Recha to this man than to any other
man in the world. But still ... Daja, you must have
patience with me for a while!

DAJA. Patience? O, Nathan, this patience of
yours, isn't it your own old harp again?

NATHAN. Grant me your patience, Daja, just a few
days longer! But look! Who's coming toward us?
Isn't it a friar? Go, Daja, ask him what he wants!

DAJA. What can he want, I wonder?
                    (She goes to him and asks.)

NATHAN. Give him what he asks, whatever he may
want! — (Aside) If only I could sound this Templar
out more closely and yet not make him curious why I'm
questioning him! Above all, I must not betray to him
just what my motive is! If my suspicion should by any
chance prove groundless, why then I've risked my
father's right to Recha all in vain! — (Loud) What
does the friar want?

DAJA. He wants to talk to you.

NATHAN. Very well, Daja! Tell him to come here
to me!

Scene vii

[NATHAN and the FRIAR]

NATHAN. (Aside) How I'd like to have remained
Recha's father! In fact, why can't I still remain
just that, even though I lose the name of father? I
know she'd surely want me as her father forever and a
day, if she only knew the joy that it would give me. —
(To Daja) Leave us now, Daja! — (To the Friar) What
can I do for you, good friar?

FRIAR. Oh, really not so very much! I'm very
pleased to find my wise friend Nathan well.

NATHAN. I take it, then, you know me?

FRIAR. Certainly I know you, Nathan! Tell me,
who doesn't know you? Your charity and generosity
have left their mark on many men and on me they've
left it over many years.

NATHAN. (Reaching for his purse) Come here,
friar, come nearer! I'll leave my mark on you again!

FRIAR. I thank you, Nathan. From a poorer man,
I — who represent the Church — would merely steal
it! I — who represent the Church — must think that
nothing I should be ashamed of! But, Nathan, try to
remember, if you can, the name I go by. You see, I
too can boast that I've likewise left my mark on you
by placing something in your hands that's not to be
despised.

NATHAN. You must forgive me, but — I'm ashamed
to say ... Tell me, please, what was it? As my atone-

ment I'll give you seven times its value.

FRIAR. Very well! But first you'll have to hear
the reason why this very day the pledge which I entrusted to your care came to my mind again.

NATHAN. The pledge which you entrusted to my
care? I don't understand.

FRIAR. Not long ago I passed my days a hermit on
Quarantana near Jericho. One day a robber band of
Arabs swooped down upon me, breaking down my little
chapel as well as my poor cell. Then, adding insult
to injury, they dragged me off with them, their prisoner. By sheer good luck I managed to escape. I came
down here straight to the Patriarch to beg him for
permission to settle in another place of solitude, a
place where I can worship God in peace until my quiet
end.

NATHAN. Please, make it short, good friar! I'm
on pins and needles! What's this all about, this
pledge? The pledge you claim that you've entrusted
to me!

FRIAR. All in good time, friend Nathan. Now,
where was I? Oh, yes, I know. Well, the Patriarch
promised me a spot on Tabor as soon as one is vacant.
In return he asked me to stay here in the meantime,
here in the cloister as a lay brother. So here I am,
my friend, and yearn a hundred times each day for
Tabor. For, you see, as long as I am here the Patriarch keeps sending me on errands that fill me with
disgust. Take, for instance, what he's ...

NATHAN. Good friar, let's get on with it! Please,
get to the point!

FRIAR. Hold your horses, Nathan! I'm coming to
it now! Today someone's whispered in the Patriarch's
ear that in this area there lives a Jew, who's raised
a Christian girl as his own Jewish daughter.

NATHAN. (Taken aback) What's this I hear?

FRIAR. First hear me out, friend Nathan. The
Patriarch has ordered me to find this Jew at once and
spare no effort to track him down. I'm telling you,
Nathan, he was beside himself with rage. He looks
upon this act as a terrible sacrilege, a sin against
the Holy Ghost, which cannot be forgiven. He believes
this sin to be the greatest of all sins, although —
thank Heaven — he's not exactly sure just why it is a
sin. Well, as he ranted on this way, my conscience
woke and suddenly I saw the light. It occurred to me
that I myself once in the past might also have commit-
ted such a mortal sin! Tell me, friend Nathan, if I'm
right! Didn't a groom once bring a little daughter
three weeks old to your house just eighteen years ago?

NATHAN. What do I hear? What's that you're saying? Well, frankly — yes, it's true.

FRIAR. Nathan, look at me closely! I'm that
groom!

NATHAN. You, friar? You?

FRIAR. Yes, Nathan! Yes, it's true! The noble-
man who gave the little girl to me, the one I brought
to you, was — if I'm not mistaken — a certain Wolf
von Filnek.

NATHAN. You're right! That's who it was!

FRIAR. Her mother died in childbirth and her sad

father suddenly was ordered to march in an attack on
Gaza. Of course, he couldn't take the tiny infant
with him, and so he asked that she be sent to you.
Don't you remember, Nathan? I met you in Darun!

NATHAN. That's right, quite right!

FRIAR. I'd hardly wonder if my memory were to
fail me! I've had so many masters and I served that
particular one for so short a term! Right after that
he lived in Ascalon. To me he always was a kind and
worthy master.

NATHAN. Yes, I agree with you. He was a man!
I've much to thank him for, for time and time again
he saved my head from the deadly spear.

FRIAR. Excellent! Because of that, no doubt, you
took his new-born child more willingly into your
house!

NATHAN. That — I assure you — is the truth!

FRIAR. Well, then, where's the child now? Don't
say the girl is dead! I hope sincerely she's not
dead! If only no one knows what passed between us!
There are other ways to get around this matter.

NATHAN. What are these other ways you have in
mind?

FRIAR. Well, Nathan, you must trust me! This is
the idea, the defense, I've planned out in my mind.
If the good I want to do comes too close to what is
evil, why then I certainly prefer not to carry out
this so-called good deed. In my opinion, we can recognize with little doubt what's evil, but not at all as
easily what's good. It was, of course, quite natural

if you planned to raise the Christian child both well
and happily, you had to raise her as your own, a Jewess. There's nothing wrong in that! Is that the
thanks you get for all your pains, your faithful love,
your fatherly care? That certainly doesn't seem right
to me! On the other hand, Nathan, in my opinion it
would have been much wiser, much more prudent, on your
part to hire someone else to raise this little Christian girl in her own Christian faith. But then, of
course, you could not have given your great love to
your friend's dear child. And tiny infants do need
love, you know, in their first tender years, even
though it be the love of a wild beast. Yes, Nathan,
they need our love even more than they need our
Christianity. There's always time for her to regain
her Christian faith. If only the girl grows up before our eyes sound both in body and in mind, then in
the sight of God she still remains what she was first.
And, after all is said and done, hasn't the Christian
doctrine been built upon the Jewish? I've often been
distressed to tears to think that many Christians can
so utterly forget that Our Dear Saviour was a Jew!

NATHAN. Good Brother, you must plead for me if
hate and hypocrisy should rise up against me for this
one act of mine, for this one decision on my part!
You alone must know the truth, but you must take my
secret with you to the grave! Up to now I've never
let my vanity persuade me to tell this tale to any
other man. To you I tell it now, for you're a pious,
simple man. I'm convinced, you see, only a simple man
can really appreciate what I'm about to say. Only
such a man as you can understand the marvelous reward
the godly man may earn for loving deeds.

FRIAR. This tale, I see, is moving you to tears.

NATHAN. No doubt, you will remember that you met

me with the child at a place called Darun. What you
probably don't know is that three days before in Gath
the Christians slaughtered every Jew, yes, every man
and woman and even every child. You probably don't
know that among the dead were found my dearest wife
and my seven sons, the hope of my old age. They'd
taken refuge in my brother's house, and all were
burned alive when the house was set afire!

    FRIAR. O, God! O, my God!

    NATHAN. When you came along, my friend, I'd been
lying in the dust and ashes before God, weeping for
three days and three nights. Did I say "weeping"?
No, no, I did much more! I pleaded, argued out my
loss with God, I raged, I stormed, I cursed myself
and all the world! I swore an oath of unrelenting
hatred for all Christians and their faith!

    FRIAR. That I can well believe!

    NATHAN. But gradually the voice of reason *did*
come back to me and whispered softly in my ear: "God
watches still! This, too, is the decree of God! So,
Nathan, practice what you've understood so very long.
To practice what you preach is certainly no harder than
it is to understand the principle involved, if only
you'll agree to do it. So, Nathan, rise up, come,
rise up!" I rose and in my anguish I then cried to
God: "I will, O Lord, I will! If that be Your will,
my God, I will!" And, good friar, at that very instant you dismounted and handed me the infant wrapped
up in your mantle. What you told me then and what I
answered I can't remember anymore. But this I *do* remember — I took the child, I laid her on my couch, I
kissed her soft cheek and, kneeling on the ground, I
sighed: "O God, for seven You already give me one!"

FRIAR. O Nathan, Nathan! You are a Christian!
By Heaven, you're a *Christian*! A truer Christian
never was!

NATHAN. It surely is a happy union for us both,
good friar, that what in your view makes me a Christian in mine makes you a Jew! But let's not weaken
our mutual trust in each other's faith by thinking in
this manner. Now we must act! Though a sevenfold
love has bound me so securely to this lovely orphaned
girl, though the very thought already kills me that in
losing her I lose again my sons — if Providence demands that I must give her up, good friar, I obey!

FRIAR. That's settled then! The course I hoped
I might suggest that you should follow, that course
your wisdom and your own good heart have already
chosen!

NATHAN. But no rash upstart must ever try to tear
her from me!

FRIAR. No, Nathan, God forbid, certainly not
that!

NATHAN. Whoever that may be, if he's got no
greater right than I, must have at least a prior right
to Recha.

FRIAR. Quite true!

NATHAN. A right which blood and nature give.

FRIAR. You're absolutely right, I think the same
as you.

NATHAN. Well, then, name the man who's related to
her more closely by blood ties — a brother, uncle, or

a cousin! Only to such a man will I consent to give
her up, this girl brought up and taught to be the
ornament of any house or any faith on earth! I hope,
good friar, you know more than I about your master,
Recha's father, and his kin.

FRIAR. Nathan, to tell the truth, I don't, for
I've already told you how short a time I served him.

NATHAN. Yes, but I'm sure you know her mother's
family and her race. Wasn't she a Stauffen too?

FRIAR. Quite possible. In fact, I think she was.

NATHAN. Didn't she have a brother, Conrad von
Stauffen, who was a Templar?

FRIAR. Yes, yes, if my memory serves me right,
she did! But wait a moment! It just occurs to me
I've still got a little book belonging to my master.
I took it from him as a keepsake when he was laid to
rest in Ascalon.

NATHAN. Well, what of that?

FRIAR. It's a little prayer-book, a breviary, we
call it. It seemed to me a book a Christian man might
use, although I — I can't read a word of it.

NATHAN. That's beside the point. Tell me more
about this book.

FRIAR. In this little book, you see, on the first
page and the last, he's written down in his own hand
the names of all his kin.

NATHAN. O, good friar, what blessèd news! Please
go at once and bring this little book to me. I'll buy

it from you and pay you for it with its weight in
gold! And, dear friend, I'll add a thousand thanks
to you! Please hurry! Run! I'm all impatience just
to see this little book!

FRIAR. Willingly, Nathan, but all my master wrote
in it is in Arabic. (Leaves)

NATHAN. That matters not a bit. Just bring it
here, good friar. O, God! If only I might still
keep my darling Recha and, in addition, win a son-in-
law like him! Who can have made it possible for the
Patriarch to know? I wonder? Can it be Daja? I
mustn't fail to ask!

Scene viii

[DAJA and NATHAN]

DAJA. (Entering in haste, excited) Nathan, just
think!

NATHAN. Yes, Daja? What's the matter now?

DAJA. Poor Recha was terribly alarmed when she
was summoned ... She's been asked to come ...

NATHAN. What's this? Who sent for her? The Patriarch?

DAJA. No, Nathan, Princess Sittah, the Sultan's
sister.

NATHAN. Not the Patriarch?

DAJA. No, Nathan, it was Sittah. Don't you understand? Princess Sittah has sent a message asking her to come.

NATHAN. Who's to come to her? Recha? Well, if Sittah's sent for her and not the Patriarch ...

DAJA. Why bring him into it?

NATHAN. Tell me, Daja, haven't you heard from your Patriarch lately? Haven't you really? Or haven't you confided something to him?

DAJA. I? Confided in him?

NATHAN. Where are the messengers?

DAJA. They're waiting outside.

NATHAN. Well, for safety's sake I'll talk to them myself. Daja, you come with me! If only nothing sinister lurks behind all this in which the Patriarch plays a leading role. (Leaves)

DAJA. As for me, my fear is altogether different! The only daughter of a Jew as rich as Nathan would be no bad match even for a Moslem. The affair with the Templar, that's all over unless I can bring myself to dare the second step and tell the dear girl who she really is. Take courage, my heart! The next time I'm alone with her I'll use the opportunity to the best advantage! Why, I'll do it now — at once — when I go with her to see what Sittah wants. A hint at least — dropped at random — can do no harm. Yes, yes, I'll do just that and right away! It's now or never! So, I'll take heart! Now onward to my task! (Follows Nathan)

END OF ACT FOUR

ACT FIVE

Scene i

[Scene: The room in Saladin's palace, to which the sacks of money have been brought and where they are still lying. SALADIN, and soon after that several MAMELUKES.]

SALADIN. (Entering) Well, there's the gold still where they set it down. But no one knows where Al-Hafi's to be found. He's likely concentrating some-where on a game of chess, oblivious even of himself, so why should he think of me? Well, I'll just be patient till he comes! But what's up now?

MAMELUKE. The news you want to hear, O Sultan! Sire, it's joyous news! The caravan's arrived from Kahira. It's finally reached us safely here with several years' tribute gathered from the wealthy Nile.

SALADIN. That's music to my ear, my Ibrahim! You are a welcome messenger indeed! At last! At last! Your Sultan thanks you for the good news you bring.

MAMELUKE. (Waiting) (Aside) Well then, let's get on with it.

SALADIN. O, you're waiting still? You may go now.

MAMELUKE. With nothing more than that to show your thanks?

SALADIN. What's that you're saying?

138

MAMELUKE. You're not inclined, I see, to tip the
messenger! So, I'm the first that Saladin rewards
with words! Well, anyhow, that in itself is something to remember! To be the first to see great Saladin a cheap skate!

SALADIN. Take one of those sacks over there!

MAMELUKE. No, not now! Perhaps you'll change
your mind and give them all to me.

SALADIN. How proud you are! Come here! There's
two for you. -- Are you really serious? Are you going?
Is it your aim to shame me in your magnanimity? I realize, of course, it costs you much more to decline
than me to give. O, Ibrahim! What unlucky fate
should misguide me in so short a time to change my
nature before I leave this earth? Is Saladin not to
die as Saladin? Why, then, he mustn't live as Saladin!

SECOND MAMELUKE. Greetings, O Sultan!

SALADIN. If you came here before me to announce ...

SECOND MAMELUKE. The caravan from Egypt has arrived!

SALADIN. That I know already.

SECOND MAMELUKE. O, then I came too late?

SALADIN. Why too late? For your good-will, go
take a sack or two.

SECOND MAMELUKE. Won't you make it three?

SALADIN. Well, well! I see that you can count!
Take them, they are yours!

SECOND MAMELUKE. There's still a third one coming, if he's able to come.

SALADIN. What do you mean? Why shouldn't he be able?

SECOND MAMELUKE. Why shouldn't he be able? Likely he broke his neck! The three of us were watching closely at the water gate and no sooner did we see the caravan than each of us leaped up and ran with all his might up the long road. The lead man fell. Then I became the leader and kept the lead until we reached the city. There Ibrahim, the rascal, knows every street and alley better than I do and so arrived here first.

SALADIN. O, the poor man fell! Perhaps he's hurt! Please go, my friend, ride out, take care of him!

SECOND MAMELUKE. I'm on my way and, if he's still alive, I'll gladly give him half these sacks as his reward! (Leaves)

SALADIN. You see, what a gallant, noble scoundrel even this man is! Who else can boast to have such Mamelukes? Why shouldn't I claim that my example helps them act the way they do? Perish the thought that in the end they form the habit of getting what they want in quite a different way!

THIRD MAMELUKE. Greetings and salutations, O Sultan!

SALADIN. Are you the man who fell?

THIRD MAMELUKE. No, my lord, I come to let you know that Emir Mansor, the leader of the caravan, has now dismounted.

SALADIN. Tell him to come in! Ah, here he is
already!

Scene ii

[EMIR MANSOR and SALADIN]

SALADIN. Welcome, good Emir! Tell me, how has
it all gone off? O, friend Mansor, we've waited long
and anxiously for you to come ...

MANSOR. This letter tells you all. Your captain,
Abdul Kassem, first had to stop by force the unrest in
Thebais before we could set out on our journey to your
land. I then came with all haste on this long march.

SALADIN. I know you did! And now, good Mansor,
you'll not mind, I'm sure, an extra chore. Proceed
without delay, collect another escort and go at once
to Lebanon to bring the greater part of this rich
treasure to my father's stronghold there.

MANSOR. I'll gladly carry out this wish of yours.

SALADIN. Be sure your escort's not too weak!
Things are no longer safe in Lebanon. Perhaps you
haven't heard? The Templars are once more afoot, so
be on your guard! But come — where have you left the
caravan? I must see it and get the new trip underway.
Then I go to Sittah.

Scene iii

[The palm grove near Nathan's house, where the TEMPLAR
is walking up and down]

TEMPLAR. I won't go in his house! My mind's made
up, I won't! He'll certainly show up, he's bound to
come! How quickly, with what pleasure, they used to
watch me at this very spot! I may still survive it if
only he'll stop hunting me as he used to do whenever I
came near. Hm! I'm very much annoyed. Why do I feel
bitter? He did say *yes* and he's never denied me anything yet. Saladin's also given me his promise to get
him to agree. Can it be the Christian has deeper
roots in me than the Jew in him? Who can really know
himself? Why should I otherwise begrudge him the
trifling prey he once took such pains to stalk and to
ensnare, poaching on Christian territory? Ah, that
was no trifling prey! It was a noble creature! A
creature, yes, but whose? Surely not the slave's who
set afloat the mere block on life's barren shore and
then went on his way and disappeared! Surely it was
the artist's rather, who in that abandoned block be-
held in his mind's eye the godlike form that he has
molded from it. Thus Recha's true father, regardless
of the Christian who begot her, still remains to all
eternity this Jew. When I think of her as a Christian
girl and nothing else, without the graces which only
such a Jew could have bestowed on her, what could my
heart have found to please it so? Probably nothing
and certainly very little! Even her smile would then
be nothing more than the soft, pretty quiver of a
muscle, and possibly that which makes her smile would
not be worth the charm in which it clothes itself upon
her lips. No, not even her smile! I've seen it wasted

with even greater charm on idle jest and folly, on
mockery, on flatterers and on wicked wooers! Did it
also charm me then? Did it inspire in me then the
wish to fritter my life away in its sunshine? I
wouldn't know. And now I am at odds with the very
man who gave this higher value to this girl! Now, why
should that be so? What if I really do deserve
Saladin's mocking laugh when he dismissed me! It's
bad enough that Saladin should think so ill of me!
How petty, how despicable, I must have seemed to him!
And all that merely for a girl? Curt, Curt, this
won't do at all! You must, you must get back on the
right track again! Suppose what Daja's told me were
merely idle gossip and difficult to prove, what then?
— See, there he comes at last out of his house en-
grossed in eager conversation! And, with whom? With
him, with my good friend the friar! Well, then he
certainly knows all about it and probably he's been
betrayed already to the Patriarch. Alas, what mis-
chief have I caused in my stupidity and my perversity!
To think that one tiny spark of passion can so inflame
our brain! Be quick about it, Curt, you must now decide at once what's to be done! I'll step aside a
bit and wait. Perhaps the friar will soon leave him
to himself.

Scene iv

[NATHAN and the FRIAR]

NATHAN. (Approaching) Good friar, please accept
my sincerest thanks.

FRIAR. And you, sir, please accept mine too.

NATHAN. I? Accept *your* thanks? What for? Because I — in my stubbornness — tried to force on you what you cannot use? You'd have every reason to thank me if your will had yielded, but you were firm in your determination. You didn't wish to be a richer man than I!

FRIAR. Besides, the book doesn't belong to me. It's the daughter's property, her sole paternal heritage. She has you, of course, and God forbid that you should ever have reason to repent all the good you've done for her.

NATHAN. Never, good brother! You need never have any fear of that.

FRIAR. Of course, I won't. But don't forget, the Templars and the Patriarchs ...

NATHAN. Try as they may, they can't make me regret anything I've ever done for Recha. Let's not even think of that! But tell me, are you sure a Templar put your Patriarch on the scent?

FRIAR. Who else could it be? A Templar talked to him just now, and what I hear seems to confirm it.

NATHAN. There's only one in all Jerusalem, and I know the man. He's a friend of mine, a young man who's both frank and noble.

FRIAR. Very true. He's the very man. But then, of course, there's quite a difference in what a person really is at heart and what the world makes him appear to be.

NATHAN. That — sad to say — is true! But whoever it may be, let him dare his best or do his worst!

Good brother, with your book I'll now defy them all!
I'm going with it directly to Saladin.

FRIAR.   God be with you, Nathan! Now I must
leave.

NATHAN.   What? Without even seeing her? Well,
come again, come soon and often. If only the Patriarch learns nothing of this matter. But if he does,
what can it matter? Today reveal to him anything you
wish.

FRIAR.   Not I, Nathan, you can depend on that.
I'm going now. (Leaves)

NATHAN.   (Alone) O, good brother, don't forget
us! O God, I could fall down upon my knees here on
this spot under the open heavens! To see at last this
threatening knot, which for so long a time has been my
secret fear, become untangled of its own accord! How
lighthearted and happy I feel now, now that there's
nothing more in this wide world I need to hide! From
this time onward I'm as free to walk erect before my
fellow-men as in Thy sight, O Lord! For God alone
needs not to judge a man according to his deeds, as
men must do, deeds which so seldom are his own!

                        Scene v

[NATHAN and the TEMPLAR, coming forward from the side
to meet him]

TEMPLAR.   Wait, Nathan, wait for me! I'm coming
with you.

NATHAN. What's that? Oh, my young friend, it's you! I thought I'd meet you at the Sultan's palace. Where have you kept yourself?

TEMPLAR. We must have missed each other. I hope you're not displeased.

NATHAN. I'm not, my friend, but Saladin ...

TEMPLAR. You had just left him when ...

NATHAN. So you did see him and speak to him! That's quite all right then.

TEMPLAR. But now he'd like to speak to us together.

NATHAN. So much the better! Well, come along then, I'm on my way to see him now.

TEMPLAR. Say, Nathan, may I ask, who was that man who just now left you?

NATHAN. Oh, don't you know him?

TEMPLAR. Wasn't it the honest friar, the one the Patriarch uses so often to do his dirty work?

NATHAN. That could well be. He's living with the Patriarch.

TEMPLAR. It's certainly a clever scheme to send this friar — simplicity personified — to clear the way for his treacherous and unholy villainy.

NATHAN. That's only true if he employs a fool and not a pious man.

TEMPLAR. The Patriarch won't trust a pious man.

NATHAN. For this man I can vouch! He'll not as-
sist the Patriarch in any wicked scheme!

TEMPLAR. That's what he'd like us to believe!
But didn't he mention *me* at all?

NATHAN. Mention *you*? Well, not exactly by your
name. In fact, he hardly knows your name.

TEMPLAR. That's very likely!

NATHAN. He did say something about a certain Templar though ...

TEMPLAR. What? What did he say?

NATHAN. Something which by no stretch of the ima-
gination can mean you, my friend.

TEMPLAR. Who knows? Nathan, I'd like to know
just what he said.

NATHAN. He told me that a Templar had accused me
to the Patriarch.

TEMPLAR. Accused, you say? Accused *you*? I must
now accuse *him* of having told a lie! Believe me,
Nathan, I'm not the sort of man to deny his deeds.
What I've done, I've done! Nor am I one who invari-
ably defends everything he does as right. Why should
I be ashamed and be condemned for owning up to one
sole fault when I've firmly made up my mind to make
it good?   I know right well what a sincere repentence
can do in order to advance a man in time to come.
Well, then, Nathan, hear me out! I am, in fact, the
Templar mentioned by the friar. Yes, I'm the man

who's guilty of accusing you. No doubt, you know very
well what it was provoked me and made my blood boil in
my veins, fool that I was! I came resolved to throw
myself into your arms with all my heart and soul. But
what was my reception? What was your reaction, Nathan?
Cold? No, even worse, lukewarm — which is far worse
than cold! How intent you were to put me off with
cautious, formal words! What great effort you exerted
to evade my questions by asking questions of your own
about my parents and God knows what else! Even now I
can't think about these things and still stay calm!
But hear me out, good Nathan! In my angry mood, Daja
came to me and whispered in my ear your secret which
cleared up the mystery. I realized then that this was
the key to your strange behavior toward me.

NATHAN. How so? What do you mean by that?

TEMPLAR. One moment, Nathan! You must bear with
me and hear me to the end. I felt that you would not
be willing to lose again to a Christian the treasure
you had stolen from the Christians. And so I thought
I'd settle this awkward problem for good and all by
putting the knife directly to your throat.

NATHAN. For good and all! What's good about it?

TEMPLAR. Nathan, please listen to the end!
There's no doubt at all about it, I did wrong. You're
likely not to blame in any way. That silly Daja perhaps has no idea what she's saying. She's openly
against you in this dangerous business and she's trying to entangle you by twisting this net around you.
And yet — it may be so, it may be true! I'm a poor
fool who's always merely ranting — now at this extreme, now that, doing far too much or far too little ...
This also may be so! Forgive me, Nathan!

NATHAN. Well, of course, if that is your opinion
of me ...

TEMPLAR. To make a long story short, Nathan, I
went to the Patriarch, but I didn't mention your name.
I repeat, whoever says I did is lying. I merely told
him of a hypothetical case, a case like yours, to
sound him out, to learn what he would do. I realize
all too clearly now even that should have been left
unspoken. It would have been much better, for didn't
I well know the Patriarch to be a wicked subtle scoundrel? Why didn't I first come to you and call you to
account? Why expose the poor girl to the danger of
losing such a father? How did it turn out? The Patriarch, true to form, by his villainy, has brought me to
my senses with a jolt. But, Nathan — listen, please,
and bear me out — suppose he knows your name, what
can he do? Only if the girl be *yours* alone and no one
else's daughter, can he take her from you. Only from
your house can he drag her off into a convent. Well
then, Nathan, give her to me, simply give her to me.
Then let him come! Just let him try to take my wife
from me! I beg you, Nathan, give her to me now,
whether she's your daughter now or not, whether she's
a Jewess or a Christian or neither, that matters not
a bit! Neither now nor ever again will I question you
about this matter, whatever the truth may be!

NATHAN. You seem to think it very necessary, I
see, for me to hide the truth?

TEMPLAR. Think as you wish.

NATHAN. I've never denied the truth to you or to
any man, who had the right to know, that she was born
a Christian child, and that the girl is my adopted
daughter. Then why, you ask, haven't I discovered it
to her? Concerning that, I'm responsible to her alone

and only to her need I apologize.

TEMPLAR. There's no need of that, even to her.
Let her never see you in a different light than now.
Spare her even now from this discovery. She's yours
still and yours alone to deal with as you wish. O,
Nathan, I beg you, please give her to me, for I alone
can and will save her for you a second time.

NATHAN. You could have, yes, you could have, but
you no longer can! Now it's too late!

TEMPLAR. I don't understand you, Nathan. Why too
late?

NATHAN. Thanks to the Patriarch!

TEMPLAR. Thanks to the Patriarch? What for? Why
give thanks to him? What has he done that we should
give him thanks?

NATHAN. We know now who her relatives are and to
what family she must be restored.

TEMPLAR. Any thanks due to the Patriarch I'll
leave to those he's helped.

NATHAN. You realize, of course, it's from those
you must receive her now, not from me.

TEMPLAR. Poor Recha! Why must Fate heap all these
hardships on your head? What would have been a blessing for other orphans becomes your evil destiny. Tell
me, Nathan, where are these new relatives of Recha's?

NATHAN. You ask me where they are?

TEMPLAR. And who they are?

NATHAN. There is a brother, in particular, who's been found. You must now ask him for Recha's hand.

TEMPLAR. A brother? What is this brother? A soldier? A churchman? Let me hear what I can hope from him.

NATHAN. As far as I know now he's neither a soldier nor a churchman. I don't believe he's either one or the other. You see I don't know him very well as yet.

TEMPLAR. What else?

NATHAN. He's an honest man. Our Recha will be very comfortable and feel quite at home with him.

TEMPLAR. And he's a Christian, of course! Nathan, at times I don't know what to make of you! Please don't take offense! Won't she now have to play the Christian — among Christians? Won't she at last become the character she's been playing for so long? Won't the weeds now finally choke up the pure wheat you have sown? And yet, in spite of that, you still can say that she'll be comfortable and feel quite at ease with her new-found brother?

NATHAN. That's what I think and hope. And if she's lacking anything with him, can't she fall back on you and me, her friends?

TEMPLAR. What will she lack with him? Won't this dear brother of hers provide his little sister richly enough with food and clothing, with luxuries and sweets? What more, I ask you, can his little sister want? Oh, yes, of course, a husband too! Well, in good time, her dear brother will, no doubt, find a husband for her too, the best that can be had!

Such a man is always to be found, you know! The
greater Christian, the better husband! — O, Nathan,
Nathan! What a perfect angel you've formed in Recha,
who now in others' hands may easily be marred!

NATHAN. Have no fear of that. That angel, I am
sure, will still prove worthy of our love.

TEMPLAR. Don't say that of *my* love! Don't say
that! *My* love won't suffer any change at all in her,
however small it be. Not even in her name! But, hold!
Does she suspect, I wonder, what's going on and what's
in store for her?

NATHAN. It's possible, though I have no idea what
her source might be.

TEMPLAR. It doesn't matter! In any case, she
shall, she must first learn from me the fate that
threatens her and is in store for her. I've changed
my mind never to see her, never to speak to her again,
till I may call her mine. I'm on my way.

NATHAN. Wait a moment! Where are you going so
fast?

TEMPLAR. To her! I must discover now if she's
got sufficient courage in her heart to follow the only
course now left open to her.

NATHAN. What course?

TEMPLAR. This one: From this time on to pay no
more attention either to you or to her brother ...

NATHAN. And what then?

TEMPLAR. ... And follow me, even if she'll be the

wife of a Moslem by doing so!

NATHAN. Wait! You won't find her! She's with
Sittah now, with the Sultan's sister.

TEMPLAR. Since when? Why?

NATHAN. And if you'd care to see her brother
there with them, then come with me.

TEMPLAR. Her brother? Whose brother? Sittah's
or Recha's?

NATHAN. Both, perhaps. Just come with me!
Please, come with me!

                              (He leads him away.)

                    Scene vi

[Sittah's harem. SITTAH and RECHA in conversation]

SITTAH. How pleased I am to meet you, my sweet
girl! But don't be so reserved, so shy and timid! Be
cheerful, be relaxed and confidential!

RECHA. Princess ...

SITTAH. No, no! That will never do! Not Princess! Call me Sittah, your friend, your sister! Call
me dear mother, for I might be almost that to you! So
young, so good, so clever! How much you know! How
much you must have read!

RECHA. How much I've *read*! Sittah, now you're
making fun of your foolish little sister. Why, I can
hardly read.

SITTAH. What, fibber? You hardly know how to read?

RECHA. My father's taught me a little. I thought you were speaking about books.

SITTAH. So I was, dear child! Of books!

RECHA. Well, I find books really hard to read! —

SITTAH. Are you in earnest?

RECHA. In full earnest! My father, you see, has little respect for that cold book-learning that's impressed upon the mind by lifeless signs.

SITTAH. What's that you're telling me? Well, he's probably quite right in that. So, all the things which you now know ...

RECHA. I've learned them from my father's lips and for most of them I could even tell you how, where and why he taught me.

SITTAH. So all is better woven into one! So the whole soul absorbs at once the full instruction!

RECHA. But, surely, Sittah too has read little or nothing!

SITTAH. How do you know? I can't be proud and boast the contrary, for what you say is true. But how can you know that? Your reason, tell me frankly — what's your reason?

RECHA. (Aside) She's so sincere, so honest, so unspoiled, so completely, naturally her own self ...

SITTAH. Well?

RECHA. My father says books seldom leave us unaffected.

SITTAH. What a wise man your father is!

RECHA. Isn't he?

SITTAH. He always seems to hit the mark!

RECHA. Doesn't he? — And this father ...

SITTAH. What's wrong with you, my dear, what ails you now?

RECHA. This father ...

SITTAH. O God, you're weeping!

RECHA. And this father — my father — it must come out! My heart is breaking — give me air — I'm fainting —
                    (Throws herself, overcome with tears, at
                                        Sittah's feet.)

SITTAH. Recha, my child, tell me, please, what ails you!

RECHA. Now I must lose this — this father!

SITTAH. You? Lose him? Why must you lose him? Be calm, dear Recha! Never, never! Come, get up and tell me all about it!

RECHA. Your offer to be my friend and sister now won't be in vain!

SITTAH. Recha, I am, I am! I am your friend and

sister! But please get up! Otherwise I'll have to
call for help!

RECHA. (Controlling herself and getting up.) Oh,
you must excuse me, Sittah! Forgive me, please! —
My grief made me forget who you really are. In Sittah's
presence there must be no sobbing, no despair! Reason
alone, calm and cold, has any power over her! Only
that person who has reason on his side will win with
her!

SITTAH. Well, what of that?

RECHA. No, Sittah, my friend and sister, I beg
you, don't allow it! Don't ever permit another father
to be forced on me!

SITTAH. Another father? Forced on you? Who can
do that? Who'd want to do that, dear, who'd ever
think of doing that?

RECHA. Who? My good, my wicked Daja can think of
doing that, and she claims that she can really do it.
I don't suppose you know this good, this wicked Daja?
Well, may God forgive her — reward her! She's done
me so much good and so much harm!

SITTAH. She's done you harm? Then, surely, she
must have very little goodness in her!

RECHA. Oh, that's not so at all! She's got so
much! So very much!

SITTAH. Who is this Daja?

RECHA. She's a Christian woman who's looked after
me from childhood on, looked after me with so much
tender care, I never missed a mother's love. May God

reward her for it! But she has worried me, tormented me, as well!

SITTAH. Now why did she do that? And, tell me, how?

RECHA. As I said, the poor woman's a Christian and, out of her very love for me, she's tortured me. She's a fanatic — you know the kind — who thinks she and she only knows the universally true and only way to God.

SITTAH. Ah, now I understand!

RECHA. She's one of those who feel duty-bound to lead all those who've strayed from this one and only path back onto it. Such people feel compelled to do so, for an overpowering urge seems to drive them on so that they can't do otherwise. And who can censure them? If it's true that their way is the only one that leads to the salvation of us all, how can they calmly watch their friends go down another road which will surely plunge them into eternal ruin and damnation? Thus it is that people such as Daja can love and hate the self-same person at the same time. But not even this forces me to make such bitter complaints against her. I could have endured her sighs, her warnings, her prayers, and her threats — much longer too, and willingly! They always called up in my mind good and wholesome thoughts. And, when all is said and done, what human heart's not flattered to be held so precious and so dear — regardless who the flatterer may be — that it can't bear the thought of everlasting parting after death?

SITTAH. That's very true.

RECHA. But — but — this thing has gone too far!

I've no defense against it anymore! Patience, logic,
nothing can help me now!

    SITTAH. Why not? What is different now and who's
to blame?

    RECHA. It's what she's just now revealed to me as
truth.

    SITTAH. Revealed to you? Just now?

    RECHA. Yes, just now! On our way here we walked
near a ruined Christian temple. Suddenly she stopped,
waging an inner struggle with herself. Her eyes were
wet with tears and she looked up first to the heavens
and then at me. "Come, my dear," she said at last,
"let's take the shortcut through this temple." She
led the way. I followed and, shuddering, I let my eye
roam over the tottering ruin. Now she stopped again
and I found myself with her on the sunken steps of a
decaying altar. What a strange feeling then came over
me, when she suddenly threw herself before me! Lying
at my feet, hot tears were streaming down her cheeks
and she kept on wringing her hands in her agitated
state!

    SITTAH. O, my dear child!

    RECHA. And before the Holy Virgin, who had heard
so many prayers there and worked so many miracles, she
implored me with a look of genuine compassion, implored
me to take pity on myself! She begged me to forgive
her if she must now at least make me aware of her
Church's claim on me.

    SITTAH. Poor unhappy girl! I guessed as much!

    RECHA. I was of Christian blood, she said, and

had been baptized. I'm not Nathan's daughter and he's
not my father! — O God! My God! He's not my father! — Sittah! Dear Sittah! Once more you see me
lying prostrate at your feet ...

SITTAH. Recha! Please don't! Get up! — My brother's coming! Stand up!

Scene vii

[SALADIN, SITTAH, and RECHA]

SALADIN. What's wrong here, Sittah?

SITTAH. She's beside herself with grief! O God,
she's had a terrible shock!

SALADIN. Who is she?

SITTAH. O, come, you know ...

SALADIN. Our Nathan's daughter? What ails her?

SITTAH. Come, child, control yourself! Stand up! —
The Sultan ...

RECHA. (Dragging herself on her knees to Saladin's
feet, her head bowed to the ground) No, I won't rise!
I'll neither rise, nor look at Saladin's countenance,
nor gaze with admiration at the bright luster of eternal justice and goodness in his yes and on his brow,
unless ...

SALADIN. Stand up!

RECHA. Unless he promises me ...

SALADIN. Come, stand up! I promise ... whatever
it may be!

RECHA. I ask this one thing only — no more, no
less: to leave my father with me and me with my father.
I don't know as yet who else wants — can possibly want
— to be my father, and I don't want to know it either.
But, tell me, is it only blood that makes a father?
Only blood?

SALADIN. I see it clearly now! Tell me, my child,
who was so cruel to put such fancies in your head?
Has this matter already been fully settled, do you
know? Has it been proven true?

RECHA. I think so, yes, it must be. Daja claims
to know it from my nurse.

SALADIN. Your nurse?

RECHA. Yes, my nurse, who — on her death-bed —
felt honor-bound to trust her with the secret.

SALADIN. Oh, I see! On her death-bed? Was she
perhaps delirious? And, even if it should be true,
what of it? Certainly blood alone doesn't make a father, not by a long shot! It scarcely makes the
father of a savage beast! At most blood only gives
the first right to earn the name. So, have no fear,
my child! Do you want my advice? When the two fathers
come to quarrel over you, leave them both be, and
choose a third. Then, Recha, take me for your father!

SITTAH. Do it, Recha! Do it!

SALADIN. I'll be a first-class father, Recha.

But hold on! I've just thought of something even
better! What need have you of fathers anyway? Suppose they die, what then? But look about in time for
someone who can start with you on equal terms, who can
keep step with you in living. Don't you know of someone such as that?

SITTAH. Don't make her blush!

SALADIN. That's exactly what I'd made up my mind
to do. Blushing, you know, makes ugly women beautiful.
Well, then, won't it make the beautiful even more
beautiful? — I've asked your father, Nathan, to come
here shortly with another man. Can't you guess his
name? Come here! You will, I'm sure, permit me, won't
you, Sittah?

SITTAH. Brother!

SALADIN. So that you'll really blush before him,
my dear child, ...

RECHA. Who's coming here? Why should I blush?

SALADIN. You little hypocrite! Well then, go
pale, if you prefer, just as you will and can! —
(A slave-girl enters and approaches Sittah.) Surely
they're not here already?

SITTAH. (To the slave-girl) Good! Let them
enter! — (To Saladin) Brother, they're here now!

Scene viii

(Last Scene)

[NATHAN and the TEMPLAR: SALADIN, SITTAH, and RECHA]

SALADIN. Welcome, good friends! You, Nathan, I
must first inform that you may now send for your gold,
which I herewith return, at your convenience.

NATHAN. Sultan! ...

SALADIN. It's now my turn, I hope, to be of service to you ...

NATHAN. Sultan! ...

SALADIN. The caravan's arrived and so I'm rich
again, richer than I've been in years. — Come, tell
me what you need to undertake an enterprise that's
really big! You merchants, I well know, can never
have too much of ready cash!

NATHAN. Why talk of such a trifle first? Here I
see an eye in tears and drying them means far more to
me! (Goes to Recha) You've been weeping, Recha?
What ails you, child? You're still my daughter, aren't
you?

RECHA. O, father! ...

NATHAN. We understand each other! That's all we
need! Cheer up! Be calm! If only your heart is still
your own and no other imminent loss threatens to disturb it, then all is well! Then you haven't lost your
father!

RECHA. No, father, no other loss! No other loss
at all!

TEMPLAR. No other loss at all? Why, then I've
been cheating myself all along! What a person doesn't
fear to lose, he never thought nor wished to own.
Very well then, Nathan, very well! That changes everything! — Saladin, we've come here at your command.
But I've misled you, so I'll not trouble you any more.

SALADIN. How rash you are again, young man! Must
everything conform to *your* ideas? Must everybody
guess *your* thoughts?

TEMPLAR. Why, Sultan, you've heard and seen it
all yourself! Isn't that enough?

SALADIN. You're quite right, I've heard and seen
it all. It really is a pity you weren't more certain
of your cause!

TEMPLAR. Well, at least, I'm certain now!

SALADIN. Whoever presumes on a good deed he's
done, he takes it back. In short, what you've saved
from the fire is not your own merely because you
saved it. Otherwise, any thief, goaded on by his own
greed for loot, by braving the flames might be a hero
just like you! (He goes to Recha, to lead her to the
Templar.) Come, my dear, don't be too stern with him.
If he were less hot and proud — anything else but
what he is — he might have hesitated, might not have
saved you. You must weigh one against the other!
Come, then! Put him to shame! You do what it was up
to him to do! Confess your love for him! Offer him
your hand! And if he should refuse it or ever forget
how infinitely more you've done for him in taking this
step than he's done for you ... Indeed, what *has* he

done for you? Let himself get scorched a little! A
great sacrifice, I must say! If that's all he can do,
then he's got nothing of my Assad in him. He merely
wears his mask, he doesn't bear his heart. Come, my
dear, give him your hand ...

SITTAH. Go, dear, go! It's really very little to
show your gratitude, for you, in fact, it's nothing at
all.

NATHAN. Stop, Saladin! Stop, Sittah!

SALADIN. What now, Nathan? Are you now interfer-
ing too?

NATHAN. There's still another person who has the
right to speak.

SALADIN. Who's denying that? A foster-father such
as you unquestionably has a say in this. The first
say, if you will. As you've heard, I know the situation through and through.

NATHAN. No, Saladin, not through and through.
I'm not speaking for myself. There's another man, O
Sultan, I beg you first to hear.

SALADIN. Who is that, if I may ask?

NATHAN. Her brother.

SALADIN. Recha's brother?

NATHAN. Yes, her brother!

RECHA. My brother? Do I have a brother?

TEMPLAR. (Rousing himself from his silent, sullen

brooding) Where is this brother? Not here yet? I
was to meet him here.

NATHAN. Please be patient!

TEMPLAR. (Very bitter) He's managed to scrape
up a father for her — won't he now scheme to find a
brother for her too?

SALADIN. That's the last straw! Christian, such
a low suspicion would not have crossed my Assad's lips.
Good! Very good! Keep it up!

NATHAN. Forgive him, Sultan! I gladly pardon
him. — Who knows what in his place and at his age we
might ourselves have said and done? (Goes up to the
Templar in a very friendly manner) Naturally, good
Templar, suspicion follows close upon the heels of
one's mistrust. If you'd have trusted me with your
real name right from the start ...

TEMPLAR. What do you mean by that?

NATHAN. You're no Stauffen!

TEMPLAR. Well, then, who am I?

NATHAN. Your name's not Curt von Stauffen!

TEMPLAR. Tell me then, what is my name?

NATHAN. Your name is Leu von Filnek.

TEMPLAR. What?

NATHAN. You're shocked?

TEMPLAR. Certainly I am, and with good reason!
Who says that?

NATHAN. I do, and I've still much more to tell
you. But first of all, my friend, let me assure you
that I'm not accusing you of telling lies.

TEMPLAR. You're not?

NATHAN. You see, it may well be you've also every
right to keep the other name.

TEMPLAR. Well now, I should hope so! (Aside)
Surely God told him to say that!

NATHAN. Your mother, you see, was a Stauffen.
Her brother and your uncle, the man who brought you
up, was Curt von Stauffen. In his care your parents
left you back in Germany when — driven from their
native land by the troubled times — they came again
for refuge to this land. This Curt von Stauffen likely adopted you in place of children of his own. Tell
me, has it been long since you've come back here with
him? He's still living, I suppose?

TEMPLAR. What can I say? Nathan, you're quite
right! It's all exactly as you've told it! My
uncle's dead. I came here with the last reinforcement
of our Order. But what does all this have to do with
Recha's brother?

NATHAN. Your father ...

TEMPLAR. What's this? My father? So you knew
him too?

NATHAN. Yes, he was my friend.

TEMPLAR. He was your friend? O, Nathan, is it
possible?

NATHAN. His name was Wolf von Filnek, but he wasn't a German ...

TEMPLAR. You know that too?

NATHAN. He married a German woman, your mother. For a short time only he lived with her in Germany.

TEMPLAR. Please say no more! But Recha's brother? What about Recha's brother?

NATHAN. You're her brother!

TEMPLAR. I? I, her *brother*?

RECHA. He's my *brother*?

SITTAH. Brother and sister!

SALADIN. They? Brother and sister?

RECHA. (Goes up to him) Oh, my brother!

TEMPLAR. (Draws back) Her brother!

RECHA. (Checks herself, then turns to Nathan) It can't be! It just can't be! His heart makes no response! O God, we are imposters!

SALADIN. (To the Templar) Imposters? How does that strike you? Do you think that? Can you think so? *You*, Templar, you alone are the imposter, for everything in you is false — your face, your voice, your bearing! Nothing of these is yours! If you can't bring yourself to acknowledge such a sister, Templar, go!

TEMPLAR. (Approaching him humbly) Sultan,

please, don't you too misinterpret my amazement.
Never, I'll wager, never have you seen your Assad in a
moment such as this! I beg you, don't deny both him
and me. (Hurrying over to Nathan) You give me and
you take away, Nathan, both with full hands. But no,
you give me more, infinitely more, than you take away!
(Embracing Recha) My sister! O, my sister!

NATHAN. Blanda von Filnek.

TEMPLAR. Blanda? Blanda, did you say? Not Recha?
She's not your Recha any more? — God! You're disown-
ing her! You're giving back to her her *Christian* name!
For my sake you're disowning her! O, Nathan, Nathan!
Don't suffer for this fault of mine!

NATHAN. Suffer? What for? My children! O, my
children! For won't my daughter's brother also be my
child?

(While Nathan gives himself up to their embraces,
Saladin, uneasy and amazed, turns to his sister,
Sittah.)

SALADIN. Sittah, what do you say to this?

SITTAH. I'm very deeply moved ...

SALADIN. As for me, I feel my heart pound with
anticipation as I face an emotion which — being closer
to home — is greater still! Prepare yourself, brace
yourself for it as best you can!

SITTAH. Prepare myself for what?

SALADIN. (To Nathan) Nathan, I'd like a word
with you — (While Nathan goes to him, Sittah goes to
the brother and sister to express her sympathy, and

Nathan and Saladin speak in whispers.) Tell me,
Nathan, didn't you say before ...

    NATHAN. Say what?

    SALADIN. That their father didn't come from Ger-
many and wasn't born a German. Well then, what was
he? From what land did he come?

    NATHAN. He never confided that to me himself.
From his own lips I didn't learn a thing about his
origin.

    SALADIN. So he was no Frank, no European? No
Occidental?

    NATHAN. Oh, he readily admitted that he wasn't.
He liked to speak the Persian language best ...

    SALADIN. Persian? Persian! What more proof do
I need now? He's the man! I mean, he *was* the man!

    NATHAN. Who? Tell me, who?

    SALADIN. My brother! My Assad! Without a doubt,
it was my Assad!

    NATHAN. Well, since you've figured out this like-
lihood yourself, you'll get the confirmation from this
book! (Handing him the breviary)

    SALADIN. (Opening it and examining it eagerly.)
Oh, it's Assad's hand! His writing too I recognize
again!

    NATHAN. As yet they don't know a thing about this
little book. Now it's up to you alone to say how much
they should be told.

SALADIN. (Turning over the pages of the book, softly to Nathan) Shall I not acknowledge my brother's children — my own flesh and blood — *my* children? Shall *I* not claim them? Shall I give them up to you? (Aloud) They're ours, Sittah! Ours, both of them! They're ours! They're my brother's and your brother's children! (He runs forward to embrace them.)

SITTAH. (Following him) What do I hear? Could it be otherwise? No, no, it must be so! —

SALADIN. (To the Templar) Now, hot-head, you must love me too. (To Recha) Now, in fact, I'm really what I vowed I'd be, whether you like it or not!

SITTAH. And so am I!

SALADIN. (Turning again to the Templar) My son! My Assad! My Assad's son!

TEMPLAR. I'm really of your blood! So those dreams with which they used to rock my infancy to sleep were in the end much more than dreams! (Falling at his feet)

SALADIN. (Raising him up) Look at the rascal! Even though he had some knowledge of this matter, he would have been content to let me almost be his murderer! Ah, just wait, you rascal, you!

(Amid the silent renewal of embraces on the part of all, the curtain falls.)

END OF ACT FIVE

APPENDIX

The Parable of the Three Rings

I. The Spanish-Jewish Version

The Parable of the Three Rings has a long and interesting history, and the first non-recorded version
is thought to be of Oriental origin. As it passed
orally from one country to another over the years, it
changed both in form and in meaning, even in the versions which have come down to us. As far as is known,
the first recorded version in the Western World is
found in Spanish-Hebrew literature about 1100 A.D.,
its authorship being ascribed to a Spanish Jew during
the epoch of the Crusades. This early Jewish form of
the tale has been preserved for posterity in the
Schebet Jehuda, a collection of writings belonging to
various dates by the Rabbi Salomo ben Verga, which
appeared near the close of the fifteenth century.
Briefly this version goes as follows:

King Pedro of Arragon one day sought to entrap
a rich Jew, Ephraim Sanchus, a man famed for his
wisdom, by posing the question to him which of the
two religions, Judaism or Christianity, he deemed
superior. Don Pedro did this in order to have an
excuse for appropriating the Jew's money, no matter
what answer Ephraim might give to the question. If
he should give his own faith the preference, he
would offend the King by scorning his faith; on the
other hand, if he should admit the supremacy of the
Christian religion, he would be denying the faith
of his fathers and be obliged, in order to be con-
sistent, to abjure Judaism. At first Ephraim tried

171

to evade giving a direct answer. He replied that
the Christians and the Hebrews both had good cause
to prefer their respective religions, for had not
Jehovah led the Israelites, His chosen people, out
of captivity in Egypt into the Promised Land, and
had not the God of the Christians given His people
dominion in Europe? The Jew added that he could,
in fact, say a great deal in favor of both religions
and concluded that both he and King Pedro had every
reason to be satisfied.

But King Pedro was not satisfied with this reply.
He told the Jew what he really wanted to know was
which religion has the greater intrinsic merit,
that is, which one is better in itself. He allowed
the Jew three days to ponder his answer. Ephraim
racked his brains and finally hit upon the means
of extricating himself from the difficulty. When
he returned before the King at the expiration of
this time, he was apparently very agitated and he
explained his confusion by relating the following
anecdote:

He began by saying that a month ago a neighbor
of his, a jeweller, on the point of setting out on
a long journey, had given to each of his two sons
a precious ring to console them for his absence.
Now this morning the two brothers had come to him,
Ephraim, to consult him about the value of the two
jewels. Upon his explaining to them that they must
wait for the return of their father, the jeweller,
who alone was competent to give them a reliable
answer, they had abused and beaten him. King Pedro
declared that this unseemly conduct on the part of
the sons deserved punishment. Thereupon the Jew
replied as follows:

"Let thine ear hear what thy mouth speaketh.
The brothers Esau and Jacob, they also, have each
a precious jewel and, if thou wouldst know which

one possesses the better stone, then send a messenger to the Great Jeweller above, for 'tis He alone
who knows the difference."

    Satisfied with this answer, King Pedro dismissed
the Jew, an honored man and laden with gifts.[1]

    It should be noted, before proceeding to the next
version of the Ring Parable, that in this first form
of the tale there are only two brothers and two rings
and that the question remains undecided as to which
of the two religions, Judaism or Christianity, is the
superior one. The Jew, accustomed to persecution,
probably felt he should not venture more than to
defend his faith.

    II. The First Italian Version in the *Cento
         Novelle Antiche*

    The addition of the third religion, namely the
Moorish, to the original two, Judaism and Christianity, most likely took place in Spain, for the Mohammedan influence was even at that time still very
strong in that country. However, no record of an
actual Spanish version which includes Mohammedanism
as the third religion has been preserved. Thus
augmented, the Parable found its way into European
literature several times in the next three centuries.
But the indecision still remained until the biased
Christian transformation which followed somewhat
clouded the clarity of the earlier Spanish-Jewish
version.

    It has been claimed[2] that the next preserved ac-
count in the *Cento Novelle Antiche*, a widely-known

---

[1] Schmidt, Erich, *Lessing, Geschichte seines Lebens und seiner
Schriften*, II, 327, Berlin, 1923.

[2] Wünsche, A., *Der Ursprung der Parabel von den drei Ringen*, p. 329,
Leipzig, 1879.

twelfth-century collection of Italian *novelas* or short
tales, may possibly be the oldest since it is both the
simplest and the shortest. Number seventy-two in the
hundred tales presented is the Parable of the Rings.
This account is so like the Arragonian version described in detail above that it will not be repeated
here. The only variations are that a Sultan replaces
King Pedro and that there are three rings and three
brothers, not two. One ring is genuine and the other
two are false, the father alone knowing which one is
the true one.

III. The Version in the *Gesta Romanorum*

From the version recorded in the collection of
Italian tales, the *Cento Novelle Antiche*, the Ring
Parable next passed into the *Gesta Romanorum*, the
popular collection of Latin stories compiled about
1300. Slight differences appear in the form in which
the tale is told in the *Gesta Romanorum* in the three
versions found in the various manuscripts. One point
which should be noted in the *Gesta Romanorum* versions
is the obvious bias on the part of the Christian tran-
scriber. Here the Christian religion is clearly given
the preference over Judaism and Mohammedanism in his
prejudiced view. In one version, moreover, an additional trait appears which Lessing used: the genuine
ring possesses the power of making its owner beloved
by God and man. The English translation by Charles
Swan of the version in the *Gesta Romanorum*[3] runs as
follows:

A certain knight had three sons, and on his
deathbed he bequeathed the inheritance to his

[3]*Gesta Romanorum,*translated into English by Charles Swan, revised by
W. Hooper, No. LXXXIX, p. 161ff., London, 1904. (See also *Gesta
Romanorum,* translated by Hermann Osterley, Caput LXXXIX, *Die triplici
statu mundi,* Berlin, 1872.)

first-born, to the second his treasury, and to the
third a very valuable ring, of more worth indeed
than all he had left to the others. But the two
former had also rings; and they were all apparently
the same. After their father's death the first son
said, "I possess that precious ring of my father."
The second said, "You have it not — I have." To
this the third son answered, "That is not true.
The elder of us hath the estate, the second the
treasure, and therefore it is but meet that I
should have the most valuable ring." The first son
answered, "Let us prove, then, whose claims to it
have the preëminence." They agreed, and several
sick men were made to resort to them for the purpose. The first two rings had no effect, but the
last cured all their infirmities.

Application

My beloved, the knight is Christ; the three
sons are the Jews, Saracens, and Christians. The
most valuable ring is faith, which is the property
only of the younger; that is, of the Christians.

IV. The Version in the *Avventuroso Siciliano* by Busone da Gabbio

Chronologically, the Ring Parable is next encounter-
ed in the novel by Busone da Gabbio — a contemporary
of Dante — entitled *Avventuroso Siciliano (Sicilian
Adventures)*, which first appeared in 1311. It has not
been conclusively established whether da Gabbio borrowed his version of the Ring Parable from the Italian
work, *Cento Novelle Antiche*, or from some other source,
but most scholars agree that Boccaccio was certainly
influenced by it in his version in the *Decamerone*,
even though he made various changes of his own. In
one place especially Boccaccio definitely changed da
Gabbio's point of view. The latter, following previous versions, gives the reason why the Sultan seeks

to rob the Jew. Here he followed the common attitude
that Jews, who were hated and despised at that time,[4]
might quite justifiably and conscientiously be robbed
of their money. Boccaccio changed all that in his
version. A tolerant, broad-minded man, he abhorred
persecution and injustice. Consequently, in his story
he did not state for what purpose the Sultan needed
money and how he proposed to get it, and he also
changed his Jew into an avaricious usurer, instead of
making him a wise and noble man.

Because Busone da Gabbio remained in the main quite
faithful to previous versions, his version will not be
repeated here. He made only one really significant
change in his tale. As before, only one ring is genuine, but it is not the father who has the task of deciding which religion is the true one. That still remains undecided, as in the earliest versions, contrary
to the biased preference given to Christianity in the
Gesta Romanorum.

V.   The Version in Boccaccio's *Decamerone*

The Ring Parable probably made its way from Spain
through Southern France into Italy and thus became
known to Boccaccio and his contemporaries in the
Renaissance. The story as told by Boccaccio in the
fourteenth century in his *Decamerone*, which was the
primary source from which Lessing drew for his version
in *Nathan the Wise*, is next in order. The English
translation by John Payne[5] follows.

Saladin, the Sultan of Babylon, having in
divers wars and in the exercise of his extraordinary

---

[4]Cf. Shakespeare, *The Merchant of Venice,* and Sir Walter Scott,
Ivandoe, for corroboration regarding this attitude.

[5]Boccaccio, *The Decameron,* translated into English by John Payne,
p. 45ff., London, 1893.

munificences expended his whole treasure and having
an urgent occasion for a good sum of money, called
to mind a rich Jew, by name Melchisedech, who lent
at usuance in Alexandria, and bethought himself
that this latter had the wherewithal to oblige him,
an he would; but he was so miserly that he would
never have done it of his free will and Saladin was
loath to use force with him; wherefore, need con-
straining him, he set his every wit at work to find
a means how the Jew might be brought to serve him
in this. Accordingly he sent for Melchisedech and,
receiving him familiarly, seated him by himself,
then said to him: "Honest man, I have understood
from divers persons that thou art a very learned
man and deeply versed in matters of divinity;
wherefore I would fain know of thee whether of the
three Laws thou reputest the true, the Jewish, the
Saracen, or the Christian?" The Jew perceived but
too well that Saladin looked to entrap him in words.
Accordingly, sharpening his wits, there speedily
occurred to him that which it behooved him reply,
and he said, "My lord, the question that you pro-
pound me is a nice one, and to acquaint you with
that which I think of the matter, it behooveth me
tell you a little story, which you shall hear.

There was once a great man and a rich who,
among other very precious jewels in his treasury,
had a very goodly and costly ring, whereunto being
minded, for its worth and beauty, to do honor and
wishing to leave it in perpetuity to his descendants, he declared that whichsoever of his sons
should at his death be found in possession thereof,
by his bequest unto him, should be recognized as
his heir and be held of all the others in honor
and reverence as chief and head. He to whom the
ring was left by him held a like course to his
own descendants, and did even as his father had
done. In brief, the ring passed from hand to hand,
through many generations, and came at last into the

possession of a man who had three goodly and virtuous sons, all very obedient to their father, wherefore he loved them all three alike. The young men
knowing the usance of the ring, each for himself,
desiring to be the more honored among his folk, be-
sought his father, who was now an old man, to leave
him the ring, whenas he came to die. The worthy
man, who loved them all alike and knew not himself
how to choose to which he had liefer leave the ring,
bethought himself, having promised it to each, to
seek to satisfy all three, and privily let make by
a good craftsman other two rings which were so like
unto the first that he himself scarce knew which
was the true. When he came to die, he secretly
gave each one of his sons his ring, wherefore each
of them, seeking after their father's death to occupy the inheritance and the honor and denying it
to the others, produced his ring in witness to his
right; and the three rings being found so like unto
one another that the true might not be known, the
question which was their father's very heir abode
pending and yet pendeth.

And so say I to you, my lord, of the three Laws to
the three peoples given of God the Father, whereof
you question me; each people deemeth itself to have
His inheritance, His true Law, and His command-
ments; but of which in very deed hath them, even
as of the rings, the question yet pendeth.

Saladin perceived that the Jew had excellently
well contrived to escape the snare which he had
spread before his feet; wherefore he concluded to
disclose to him his need and see if he were willing
to serve him; and so accordingly he did, confessing
to him that which he had it in mind to do, had he
not answered him on such discreet wise. The Jew
freely furnished him with all that he required, and
the Sultan afterwards satisfied him in full; moreover, he gave him other great gifts, and still had

him to friend and maintained him about his person
in high and honorable estate.

In general, Boccaccio does not deviate greatly from
the previous Italian versions. In his account it is
no longer an indefinite Sultan, but the warlike and
heroic Saladin who, in dire need of money, summons the
wealthy and usurious Jew Melchisedech from Alexandria
to Jerusalem. He does this in order to get a loan
from him, and he "softens him up" by putting the vexa-
tious question to him which of the three religions, in
his opinion, is the true one. The Jew soon makes up
his mind what he will do and recounts to Saladin, as
if by sudden inspiration, the story of the three rings.
Boccaccio closes with the remark that each of the
three nations believes its religion to be the real,
divine revelation; but which really has the true one
can no more be decided than which is really the true
ring. As will be shown below, Lessing goes far beyond
this cut and dried conclusion in his eloquent plea for
toleration and religious concord.

VI.   The Version in Lessing's *Nathan the Wise*

Four centuries had elapsed before Gotthold Ephraim
Lessing again took up the Ring Parable and developed
it into its classic form in his *Nathan the Wise* in
1779. As the complete translation of Lessing's version of the Ring Parable is to be found in the text,
Nathan III, vii, it is not repeated here.

In line with his predecessors, Lessing likewise
modified his version in order to make it conform to
his own views of religious truth. It was chiefly from
Boccaccio's version that he drew for his own, but he
refined and expanded it so that it became much more
meaningful in his beautiful drama. His aim was not
to exalt one religion at the expense of the two others,
as had very obviously been done in the version of the
Gesta Romanorum, nor to treat all religions indifferently in the spirit of Boccaccio, but rather to inculcate

the universality of the religious impulse and its role
in the development of the human race.

In general, Lessing followed the outline of the
tale as it appears in Boccaccio's version, but he
digresses from the latter in two important points,
where he agrees with the story contained in the *Gesta
Romanorum*, namely, the ring is, first of all, from
loving hands and not a mere jewel; it possesses super-
natural power. This special virtue causes the person
who wears the genuine ring, in Lessing's version, to
find favor in the sight of God and man. However, the
ring is able to produce this effect only when the
wearer recognizes its hidden virtue, for only then
will it cause him to find favor in the sight of God
and man. Unlike Boccaccio, who in the end cuts the
story off by simply stating that the question as to
which religion is the genuine one must remain undecided just as the question as to which ring is the
genuine one remains unsolved, Lessing went far beyond
this point to reach his conclusion. When the three
sons appear before the judge, he reminds them, first
of all, of the great mystic virtue of the genuine
ring. He then concludes that none of the three rings
possesses the promised gift, since no one of the
three brothers is genuinely loved by the other two.
True virtue and true religion are manifest only in
works of love. The judge states that the question
cannot be settled at once, and that very likely their
father did not intend to discriminate between members
of his family any more.

But after the judge has dismissed the three quar-
relling sons from his court due to lack of proof to
form any valid decision, it occurs to him that there
is indeed a key to this seeming puzzle. The true
ring possesses a magic virtue which must necessarily
manifest itself in the one who possesses it and wears
it in this confidence. As no one brother possesses
the power to make himself beloved by the other two,

none has the genuine ring. He concludes that the true
ring must have been lost and that those which the
three brothers now have are false. His judicial decision is that each son must now think he has the true
ring, and each must strive to show the virtue of his
ring. He therefore urges the three sons to go forth
in harmony and vie with one another in love, and by
gentleness, good works, and devotion to God, to co-
operate with the virtue which "might be inherent" in
their rings.

From what has been said, it becomes obvious that
Lessing borrowed extensively from Boccaccio and
other sources. However, in spite of the fact that he
owes much of the outward form of his Ring Parable to
foreign sources, he has broadened and deepened its
meaning and invested it in a form of classic beauty.

Boccaccio's *Decamerone* provided Lessing with other
hints for his *Nathan the Wise*. In the Third Story of
the Tenth Day, Boccaccio portrays a noble and kind man
named Nathan and an impulsive youth named Mithridanes,
which furnished features for Lessing's Nathan and his
Templar. In his great unselfishness, at least,
Boccaccio's character Nathan bears considerable resemblance to his namesake in Lessing's drama. The
name Nathan is certainly more euphonious than Melchisedech; hence Lessing used the name Nathan and at the
same time transferred the qualities of Boccaccio's
Nathan to his own hero. Certain hints were also de-
rived from the Fifth Story of the Fifth Day and used
by Lessing. In that story Boccaccio tells of an infant girl, who was lost to her parents, brought up by
a stranger, and wooed by her own brother in later
years. Guidotta, on her deathbed, is represented as
leaving an adopted daughter to the care of a good
friend, Giacomino, who brings her up as his own child
and loves her dearly. Giannole and Minghine are both
described as being in love with her and fighting on
her account. Finally, through the complications of

this love affair, she is recognized again as Giannole's sister and is afterwards then married to
Minghine. Again in the Ninth Story of the Tenth Day
the Sultan Saladin plays a part and is represented as
exhibiting that clemency and courtesy toward his
Christian antagonists which made him so justly a popular figure in the Middle Ages. It should be noted in
passing, however, that Lessing's main authority for
the character of Saladin was M. Marin's *Histoire de
Saladin*, a comprehensive work in two volumes, published in La Haye in 1758. Finally, in addition to
the above alterations made by Lessing in Boccaccio's
Ring Parable, Story Three of the First Day, he also
represents Saladin as Sultan of Jerusalem, in accord-
ance with historical fact, instead of placing him in
Babylon; moreover, he has Nathan reside in Jerusalem
also, not in Alexandria, as in the Italian version of
Boccaccio.

On August 11, 1778, Lessing wrote in a letter to
his brother: "Turn to the *Decamerone* of Boccaccio,
Giora. I, Nov. III, Melchisedech, Giudeo. I think I
have invented a very interesting episode to it, so
that all will read well." That Lessing was not wrong
has been corroborated by the universal admiration ac-
corded his famous Ring Parable in *Nathan the Wise*.

BIBLIOGRAPHY

The bibliography here presented makes no claim to completeness. For the most part, those works consulted for the preparation of this book have been listed, particularly those in German below. The titles in English dealing with Lessing and his works, which follow immediately, have been added for the benefit of those readers who have no knowledge of German.

I. <u>References in English dealing with Lessing and his Works</u>

Anderson, John P., *Bibliography of Lessing to 1888*, London, 1889. (For German Bibliography of Lessing see Karl Goedeke, *Grundriss zur Geschichte der deutschen Dichtung aus den Quellen* and P. Strauch, *Bibliographie zur deutschen Literatur.*)

Bell, Ernest, *The Dramatic Works of G.E. Lessing*, translated from the German, London, George Bell, 1878.

Fiske, John, *The Unseen World and Other Essays*, Boston, 1880.

Garland, H.B., *Lessing, the Founder of Modern German Literature*, Cambridge University Press, 1937.

Gruener, G., "The Genesis of the Characters in Lessing's *Nathan der Weise*," in *Publications of the Modern Language Association*, Vol. VII, p. 75.

Hedge, F.H., *Hours with the German Classics*, Boston, 1886.

Herse, W., *Four Essays on Lessing*, Wolfenbüttel-Hannover, 1947.

Lowell, James Russell, *Among my Books*, Boston, 1879

Robertson, J. G., *Lessing's Dramatic Theory*,
    Cambridge, 1937.
Rolleston, T.W., *The Life of Gotthold Ephraim
    Lessing*, London, 1889.
Rolleston, T.W., *Lessing's Place in German Litera-
    ture*, London, 1895.
Sime, James, *Lessing*, 2 volumes, London, Trübner,
    1879.
Stahr, Adolf, *G.E. Lessing, his Life and Works*,
    translated into English by E.P. Evans, Boston,
    1866.
Vail, Curtis C.D., *Lessing's Relation to the
    English Language and Literature*, New York,
    1936.
Zimmern, Helen, *The Life of Lessing*, (Introduction
    in Ernest Bell, *The Dramatic Works of G.E.
    Lessing*), London, 1878.

II. References in German dealing with Lessing and
    his Works

    A. Lessing's Complete Works

        Boxberger, R., *Lessings sämmtliche Werke*,
            Deutsche-National-Litteratur, Theil 14,
            Berlin-Stuttgart, 1882.
        Göring, Hugo, *Lessings sämmtliche Werke*,
            Stuttgart, Cotta, n.d.
        Lachmann, Karl, *Kritische Gesamtausgabe
            Lessings Werke*, Berlin, 1838-40.
        Nodnagel, August, *Lessings Dramen und
            dramatische Fragmente*, Darmstadt, 1842.
        Petersen, Julius, and Olshausen, W. von,
            *G.E. Lessings Werke; vollständige Ausgabe
            in 25 Teilen*, Berlin, 1925.

    B. Lessing's Biography and Comments on his
        Writings

        Danzel, T.W., and Guhrauer, G.E., *Gotthold
            Ephraim Lessing, sein Leben und seine
            Werke*, Berlin, 1880.

Düntzer, Heinrich, *Lessings Leben*, Leipzig, 1882.

Oehlke, W., *Gotthold Ephraim Lessing*, München, 1929.

Redlich, C.C., *G.E. Lessing*, Berlin, 1884.

Schmidt, Erich, *Lessing, Geschichte seines Lebens und seiner Schriften*, Berlin, 1923.

Schmidt, Julian, *Gotthold Ephraim Lessing*, Leipzig, 1897.

Schrempf, C., *Lessings Leben*, Leipzig, 1913.

Stahr, Adolf, *G.E. Lessing, sein Leben und seine Werke*, 9. Auflage, Berlin, 1887.

Strodtmann, Adolf, *G.E. Lessing, ein Lebensbild*, Berlin, 1879.

Werner, R.M., *Gotthold Ephraim Lessing*, Leipzig, 1929.

C. <u>Lessing's Religious Controversy with Goeze</u>

Boden, August, *Lessing und Goeze, ein Beitrag zur Litteraturund Kirchgeschichte des achtzehnten Jahrhunderts*, Leipzig und Heidelberg, 1862.

Bohtz, August Wilhelm, *G.E. Lessings Protestantismus und Nathan der Weise*, Göttingen, 1854.

Eichholz, G., *Die Geschichte als theologisches Problem bei Lessing*, Bonn, 1933.

Fittbogen, G., *Die Religion Lessings*, Leipzig, 1923.

Fontanés, Ernst, *Le christianisme moderne, étude sur Lessing*, Paris, 1867.

Schmidt, Erich, "Goezes Streitschriften gegen Lessing," in *Deutsche Literaturdenkmale des 18. und 19. Jahrhunderts*, Bde. 43-45, Stuttgart, 1893. (See also Volume II, pp. 347-485 of Erich Schmidt's *Lessing*.)

Schwarz, Carl, *Gotthold Ephraim Lessing als Theologe*, Halle, Pfeffer, 1854.

Strauss, David Friedrich, *Hermann Samuel Reimarus und seine Schutzschrift für die vernünftigen Verehrer Gottes*, Bonn, 1877.

D. <u>Lessing's *Nathan the Wise*</u>

Caro, J., *Lessing und Swift; eine Studie über Nathan der Weise*, Leipzig, Abel, n.d.

Diesterweg, Adolph, *Lessings Nathan*, Berlin, 1865.

Düntzer, Heinrich, *Lessings Nathan der Weise*, Leipzig, Wartig, 1894.

Fischer, Kuno, *Lessings Nathan der Weise*, 5. Auflage, Stuttgart und Berlin, 1905.

Fürst, Julius, *Lessings Nathan der Weise; historisch und philosophisch erläutert*, Leipzig, Friedrich, 1881.

Giesse, W., *Gotthold Ephraim Lessings Nathan der Weise; ein Vortrag*, Darmstadt und Leipzig, Zernin, 1866.

Köpke, Ernst, *Studien zu Lessings Nathan; ein Vortrag*, Brandenburg a/H., Müller, 1865.

Naumann, F., *Literatur über Lessings Nathan, aus den Quellen*, Dresden, Burbach, 1867.

Niemeyer, Eduard, *Lessings Nathan der Weise*, Leipzig, Siegesmund und Volkening, 1887.

Pabst, C.R., *Vorlesungen über G.E. Lessings Nathan*, Bern, Haller, 1881.

Peters, R., *Lessings Nathan der Weise*, Leipzig, 1900.

Rönnefahrt, J.G., *Lessings dramatisches Gedicht Nathan der Weise, aus seinem Inhalte erklärt*, Stendal, Franzen und Grosse, 1863.

Spielhagen, Friedrich, *Faust und Nathan*, Berlin, Duncker, 1867.

Strauss, David Friedrich, *Lessings Nathan
    der Weise; ein Vortrag,* Bonn, Emil
    Strauss, 1877.
Stümke, H., *Die Fortsetzungen, Nachahmungen
    und Travestien von Lessings Nathan,*
    Berlin, 1904.
Trosien, E., *Lessings Nathan der Weise; ein
    Vortrag,* Hamburg, Richter, n.d.
Werder, Karl, *Vorlesungen über Lessings
    Nathan,* Berlin, W.F. Fontane, 1903.

E. The Parable of the Three Rings

Osterley, Hermann, *Gesta Romanorum,* ins
    Deutsche übersetzt, Berlin, 1872.
Paris, Gaston, *La poésie du moyen âge,*
    Paris, 1895.
Payne, J., *Boccaccio's Decameron,* translated
    into English, London, 1893.
Schmidt, Erich, *Lessing, Geschichte seines
    Lebens und seiner Schriften,* pp. 491-512,
    Berlin, 1892.
Swan, Charles, *Gesta Romanorum,* translated
    into English, revised by W. Hooper,
    London, 1904.
Wright, Thomas, *The Decameron of Boccaccio,*
    translated into English with an intro-
    duction, London, n.d.
Wünsche, A., *Der Ursprung der Parabel von
    den drei Ringen,* Leipzig, 1879.

F. Miscellaneous References for Lessing

Arx, A. von, *Lessing und die geschichtliche
    Welt,* Leipzig, 1944.
Belling, R., *Die Metrik Lessings,* Berlin,
    1887.
Bobinski, K., *Gotthold Ephraim Lessing,*
    Berlin, 1900.

Braum, Julius, *Lessing im Urteile seiner Zeitgenossen*, 3 Bde., Berlin, 1897.

Bulthaupt, Heinrich, *Dramaturgie des Schauspiels*, Leipzig, 1896.

Clivio, J., *Lessing und das Problem der Tragödie*, Zürich, 1928.

Kettner, G., *Lessings Dramen im Lichte ihrer und unserer Zeit*, Berlin, 1904.

Kinkel, H., *Lessings Dramen in Frankreich*, Darmstadt, 1908.

Klein, F., *Lessings Weltanschauung*, Wien, 1931.

Kont, J., *Lessing et l'antiquité*, Paris, 1874.

Leander, F., *Lessing als ästhetischer Denker*, Göteborg, 1942.

Lehmann, August, *Forschungen über Lessings Sprache*, Braunschweig, 1875.

Leisegang, H., *Lessings Weltanschauung*, Leipzig, 1931.

Marin, M., *Histoire de Saladin*, La Haye, 1758.

Minor, J., *Neuhochdeutsche Metrik*, Strassburg, 1893.

Oehlke, W., *Lessing und seine Zeit*, München, 1919.

Prölss, Robert, *Geschichte des neueren Dramas*, Bd. III, Leipzig, 1880.

Sauer, A., *Über den fünffüssigen Iambus von Lessings Nathan*, Wien, 1879.

Schmitz, F., *Lessings Stellung in der Entfaltung des Individualismus*, Berkeley, California, 1941.

Todt, W., *Lessing in England, 1767-1850*, Heidelberg, 1912.

Wagner, A., *Lessing, das Erwachen des deutschen Geistes*, Leipzig, 1931.

Wiese, Benno von, *Lessing: Dichtung, Aesthetik, Philosophie*, Leipzig, 1931.

Zarncke, F., *Über den fünffüssigen Iambus
mit besonderer Rücksicht auf seine
Behandlung durch Lessing, Schiller, und
Goethe*, Leipzig, 1897.

Other References Consulted after Completion of the Bibliography

Fischer, Kuno, *Gotthold Ephraim Lessing als
Reformator der deutschen Literatur*, 4.
Auflage, Stuttgart, 1896.

Hettner, H., *Litteraturgeschichte des
achtzehnten Jahrhunderts*, 4. Auflage,
Braunschweig, 1894.

Horn, F., *Lessing, Jesus, und Kant*, Wien,
1880.